a memoir

Rita Therese

ALLEN&UNWIN
SYDNEY • MELBOURNE • AUCKLAND • LONDON

Allen & Unwin
83 Alexander Street
Crows Nest NSW 2065
Australia
Phone: (61 2) 8425 0100
Email: info@allenandunwin.com
Web: www.allenandunwin.com

A catalogue record for this
book is available from the
National Library of Australia

ISBN 9781 76087502 2

Set in 12/18.5 pt Sabon LT by Midland Typesetters, Australia
Printed and bound in Australia by Griffin Press, part of Ovato

10 9 8

MIX
Paper from
responsible sources
FSC® C009448

The paper in this book is FSC® certified.
FSC® promotes environmentally responsible
socially beneficial and economically viable
management of the world's forests.

For Peter

Author's note

Whilst I have done my best to write the truth, I have also distorted it. In some instances, names have been changed or identities clouded in order for me to speak freely.

I have tried to recreate events, locales and conversations from my memories of them. In order to maintain anonymity, in some instances I have changed the names of individuals and places. I may also have changed some identifying characteristics and details such as physical properties, occupations and places of residence.

Port Hedland, 12 October 2015

As usual, I wake up at 3 p.m. I have three hours of sunlight before I have to start work again. My feet hit the cold linoleum and are immediately caked in a fine layer of red dust. There are no windows in here but the sand from the desert manages to find its way into every crevice.

When I arrived, I did my best to make the room feel like mine. The furniture was simple: a single bed, a crooked side table, and a desk that served as a vanity complete with plastic garden chair and a dusty mirror. I arranged my make-up carefully on the table and in the corner I placed my 8-inch stripper heels on top of a case of Diet Cokes. A hooker still life.

I empty my purse of the night before. Condoms, a bottle of lube, a half-chewed pack of spearmint gum, several lighters, a broken cigarette, a tube of sticky pink lip-gloss and, underneath it all, a wad of green notes. I begin to carefully unfurl the money, lay it out in front of me. I always save this part for last. It gives me a thrill to know I've underestimated my earnings. Inside a balled-up pair of dirty leggings, a place nobody would think to look, are several envelopes. This is my morning routine and it's day fifteen of working the night shift.

I have a system to get tipped. My friend taught me. When we worked at a strip club, she used to move into the lap dance room ahead of me, the smell of her perfume a trail I'd follow. Her hips would move to meet her hands and she'd cock them and say, so, do you want the fun dance or the boring dance?

Well, which one would you have picked?

I always wait until the client has showered and I make small talk as I throw the drop sheet over the double bed. The air conditioner whirrs, keeping the desert heat at bay. The showers are cold. A stranger stands in front of me, awkward and naked. I sit on the bed and pat the spot next to me.

'Come sit down and get comfortable.'

I stay in my tight dress and make them lie in the centre of the bed, propped up on the pillow. I crawl on top of them; my thighs straddle their naked cock and damp chest. My clothes stay on to make them feel vulnerable, exposed. I lean down and lick their ears, kiss their neck and say softly, 'Do you want the fun booking or the boring booking?'

'What's in the fun booking?'

'Well, you get to kiss me. You can fuck my tits and come all over my chest. You can work your way down my body and eat my pussy. You can face fuck me. I've never had anyone ask for a refund.' They hand the money over and I smile sweetly but inside I feel the rush of getting what I want, what I knew I was going to get as soon as they chose me.

When you start working like this, so far away from home, the only way to survive is to get into a routine. My routine grounds me, buffers me from any surprises. I know when I'll eat, when I'll turn on the fan in front of the dust-covered treadmill on the veranda, when I'll start fucking. My bedroom is a portable hut in a row of five; thin prefab walls separate me from the other girls rising to start their day. I am relieved this morning because the midge bites I was covered head to toe in have finally finished scabbing over. It was a full moon a few nights ago and still blazingly hot at 6 p.m., so I sat in the blow-up pool with a Corona and a cigarette and woke up the next morning covered in red welts, screaming in pain.

I open the door to my cabin and the sun burns my eyes. In the morning I'm tired. I miss my home and I miss cold breezes. The sun here is relentless, pounding. I've taken to putting my sunglasses on before I open the door.

I prefer my night routine to my morning one. When the brothel shuts at 7 a.m. and the last client leaves, it is my job to walk down the driveway and padlock the gates. I do this so I can watch the sun rise over the red earth, pouring pink and gold through the eucalyptus and scrub. I take my heels off and hike up my Lycra dress and begin to clean my workroom. I play Fleetwood Mac and hum along as I empty the condom bin and strip the sheets from the bed. I take my time as I unfold the clean linen, carefully smoothing the creases from the bed. My body is weary and my mind is gloriously blank. After the room is clean, I take myself to the shower and stand under the hot water. I picture every strained interaction, every fumble—a relentless fucking and pounding and the friction from my dry pussy against latex. I watch it gurgle down the drain with the gritty sand, lube and massage oil. Finally, when my dark eye make-up is removed and my hair is wet, I put on my boyfriend's t-shirt. It smells like him. I make a cup of tea and sit on the chair on the deck and I text him as he takes the train to work. He sends me sweet messages telling me how much he misses me and he sends me filthy messages telling me how much he misses fucking my cunt. He asks me how my night has been, and we are as normal as one could hope to be.

This afternoon, the air blows a restless northern wind and picks up grit that flies into my eyes. I remember this because when I began to sob later on, I felt the itch and sting from the dirt trapped in my cornea. I think that's what strikes people the most when something terrible happens. You remember the mundane task you were doing in equal parts bitterness and fondness. You think, my life was so damn perfect and all you were doing was stirring some instant coffee into hot water and rubbing sand from your eyes.

My phone lights up on the counter and it's my younger brother. I pick up the call and rest the phone in the crook of my shoulder. I remember that I was cracking ice cubes from a tray to place in my coffee. I remember that they melted in my hand because I forgot they were there, I forgot that ice was stuck to my skin until I unclenched my fist and saw it was wet.

The line is tinny and hollow and I'm struggling to make out what he's saying. Speak up Will, I say, but he's laughing so much he can't get the words out.

'It's James. He's dead.'

I start laughing too, and the laughter stretches down and into the hut and through the plastic-wrapped bags of wrinkled, cum-filled condoms until it becomes thin and brittle, snapping in the wind.

I get up and I'm wheezing now. The red earth is like hot glue oozing down my throat. Suddenly I don't like the open plains of Port Hedland, Western Australia. The desert that looks so beautiful in the morning light is now a prison. I am surrounded by the endless stretches of land and I just want to run across it all and into the room and cradle a blond head in my hands, get there in time so the blood is still hot.

But we just did this. We just did this with Peter. I say this and in that moment I believe it can all be undone. I can go back to my ice cubes and coffee and in ten more days I'll come home and my brothers will be alive and everything, it will be fine. It'll be just fine.

SEX

Bar Bunny

When I called the number for Bar Bunnies, I was surprised at how friendly the voice on the other end of the phone was. It was the beginning of my relationship with my sex worker 'mother' Zoe, one of many stand-in parents who would fill the widening gap between myself and my own family. I had begun to drift, the relationship with my own mother was strained and fraying. Now aged eighteen, a legal adult, I felt her presence less and less. I considered myself to be the strange one in the family, an outsider.

I walked around my studio apartment for an hour, the phone nestled in the crook of my shoulder as Zoe talked me through the A–Z of topless waitressing.

I would mostly be working on the weekend, with the occasional weekday job coming through. Jobs could be anywhere from one to eight hours long, and I would be paid an hourly rate of $60. It was my job to separate the cash for myself out of the envelope I would be given and to set aside Zoe's cut. Once a week I would deposit this into her account. Jobs that were outside the CBD, down the peninsula or out in the country were given a travel allowance. Zoe would send periodic texts of jobs and it was up to you to yay or nay them.

'Do you drive?' asked Zoe.

'No, but I can take the bus or the train, or get a cab.'

It was the middle of winter, the slower season for topless waitressing. Peak seasons were spring and summer—bucks parties, end-of-year work parties, boat cruises on the Yarra. These were the jobs where you made serious money.

'I've got a job coming up this Friday—a bucks party in Greensborough. Can you do that? It's 6–9 p.m.'

We had no drivers and no security. We went to jobs on a hope and a prayer that it wasn't a group of convicted rapists waiting for us to step through their front door.

Zoe paused.

'When you go to the job, just make sure that if anyone asks how long you've been doing this for, you say "a while". It's not good for them to know you are new. Did you want to do lappies too?'

'Lappies?'

'Lap dances. Most girls ask for $50 for three songs, but make sure you only do them when your shift has ended. Essentially, be fun, be polite and make sure you get them drinks! Also, if you have any problems, go and speak to the guy who's in charge of organising you—they are usually pretty helpful. And don't leave your money in your bag. Always keep it on you.' I thought that was everything and went to say goodbye, but Zoe had just paused to catch breath. Finally, she imparted the most important piece of advice—charge them for everything, and wear a skirt or a pair of shorts—it was $50 for me to take them off.

That Friday, I got a train and a cab and found myself in front of a suburban house. I shivered in the cold winter night air. I knocked on the front door. It swung open and a man stood there. His face lit up.

'One of the toppies is here!' he yelled out.

I found myself in a bathroom standing on a pink shagpile bathmat. Looking in the mirror, I brushed my hair, slipped out of my leggings and into my miniskirt and heels. Taking a deep breath, I unclasped my bra and placed it in my bag. My heart was pounding in my chest. I tucked my handbag under my arm and swung the door open.

The party was in the basement, and my bare boobs bounced up and down as I stepped down the stairs. I heard the catcalls and exclamations from the guys. I considered running back up, but instead I threw my head back, shot them all a beaming smile and suppressed the urge to have an anxious vomit in the corner.

At the makeshift bar stood a petite girl with long, silky brown hair and huge fake tits. She was wearing thigh-high socks and heels, and a Tiffany bracelet around her tiny, fake-tanned wrist. She looked up at me, smiled and waved me over.

I was quickly welcomed into the fold by the other Bar Bunnies. There was a level of solidarity among the girls I've never experienced doing any other kinds of sex work. Perhaps it was being thrust into these strangers' houses, where we had to band together. Or perhaps it was because we were all on an hourly rate and didn't need to hustle so hard.

The petite girl's name was Elle, and she quickly became a close friend. At a job a few weeks later, she introduced me to her best friend, Grace. I met a tall, busty, blonde Kiwi called Jessica and a curvaceous brunette called Olivia at other jobs and bonded with them too. Zoe began to book me on jobs that had at least one of my friends there and from Friday to Sunday mornings every weekend, I had the time of my life. While I had friends at the lingerie restaurant where I'd been working, I hadn't yet experienced the feeling of belonging to a community. I had found mine now.

Some of my favourite times were when Elle and I got booked on jobs down on the coast, a few hours' drive from Melbourne. I would take the tram to her place in Thornbury and climb into her 4WD, and we'd chain-smoke cigarettes and drink Red Bulls and talk about everything under the sun. We'd talk about men, heartbreak, being a woman, our jobs, our friends and our lives. The time would fly past as we sped down the highway towards Rosebud or Dromana.

Navigating a job was always a challenge. You had to assert yourself as soon as you walked through the door. You made eye contact, you kissed the clients on the cheek, or you shook their hands. You got the money and you went to the bathroom to change and when you came out, you had your game face on. You needed to command authority in a room full of ten to thirty drunk, horny guys with your tits hanging out. If you didn't set the tone when you walked in, you were fair game. Guys would grab your ass, make crude jokes, and generally try to fuck with you. This wasn't a job for the shy or the timid.

Some weekends I would have four jobs on a Friday, and four on a Saturday. I'd start drinking at 12 p.m. on a boat cruise in the Docklands, and finish drinking at 2 a.m. playing poker at somebody's house in the middle of nowhere. I was always relieved when the job somewhere in between was a bunch of Greek or Italian guys. I'd put my bag down and go out to the backyard where a *gyros* would be roasting over a coal pit, get a plastic plate and ladle it high with juicy slivers of lamb and chicken, white bread rolls and potato salad. I loved that they were always happy to feed me, and it meant I could keep up with the shots and vodka Red Bulls I'd be consuming for the rest of the night. I was practically addicted to sugar-free Red Bull at this point, and I'd smoke a pack of cigarettes by the time the night was over.

Looking back at it, I don't know how I made it to half of those jobs. Zoe would laugh at me and say, 'I love you because I could send you to Timbuktu and you'd find a way to get there.' I would sit up the night before, entering all the addresses of the apartments, houses and venues I needed to go to and find the bus or train that would take me there. Sometimes I hitched rides from the other girls, but mostly I wandered strange suburban streets, drunk, looking at Google Maps on my iPhone. One night I finished up a job in Rosebud at 3 a.m. I took a cab to Frankston station and fell asleep on the platform, woken up by my alarm at 4:45 a.m. to catch the first train of the day. I couldn't bear to part with my money over something as frivolous as a driver or a taxi.

When I first started as a Bar Bunny, the idea of not having a bra on shocked me. Within a few weeks I barely noticed I was topless. One night, Elle and I were at a job at a city penthouse. It was a small gathering, a bunch of guys playing poker and drinking beers. I turned around from making a Jack and Coke and saw Elle stroll out of the bathroom, butt naked except for stilettos. My jaw dropped.

'Vic,' I hissed at her, 'where are your clothes?'

'Chill out,' she said. 'The guys paid extra for me to go nude.' She turned back and did the nude waitress equivalent of the bunny dip—swivel your hips to the side and sit on your heels to get a beer from the Esky, so you don't flash your asshole to the entire room.

I placed the Jack and Coke down on the table in front of the guy, and he looked up from the game.

'Would you be happy to go nude as well?'

I felt a flush of anxiety and stammered out a reply, but before I knew it, I had an extra $100 in my hand and I was removing my G-string in the bathroom. I walked out feeling like I was about to have a heart attack and none of the guys even looked up from their game. Elle gave me a thumbs up and a wink from the other side of the room.

'So,' said Zoe, when she rang me a few days later for a chat, 'are you happy for me to advertise that you do nude waitressing now too?'

It was the snowball effect. Academics and anti-sex work feminists like to attribute these kinds of things to sex workers becoming desensitised to the horrors of the industry, but all that's happening is you've realised it just isn't a big deal to get your coochie out for money. You think you're going to be even more vulnerable, but the men look at you with awe. Why wouldn't they? What other badass is walking around the Hills hoist starkers, serving drinks and not batting an eyelid? Walking around a group of strangers butt naked did wonders for my social anxiety. If you can manage to hold a charming, engaging conversation with your pussy hanging out, you can talk to anyone.

But as badass as that felt, you were nothing compared to the show girls who came in. The show girls were always my favourite part of the evening.

At Bar Bunnies, we had toppies (topless waitresses) and strippers (the show girls). At a bucks party, it was usually the same deal—you'd have a couple of toppies for two to three hours, and then the stripper would show up.

The first time I ever saw a show, I was blown away.

Strip shows usually go like this. The girl struts in, in her Juicy Couture sweatpants, accompanied by a big dude clutching a blow-up paddling pool and an AUX cable. She disappears into the bathroom. The guys round each other up, with somebody yelling 'The stripper's here!' a la Pauly D's 'Cabs are here!' and they form a semicircle in the lounge room or backyard. Occasionally some forward-thinking gentleman will pull out a big blanket and lay it on the ground so the stripper doesn't end up with carpet burn, but the girls working the circuit usually come prepared with their own.

The stripper emerges from the bathroom, always in some amazing costume and always in a pair of Pleaser Heels. The burly guy sets up her paddling pool, gets the music ready and stands at the back of the room, arms folded across his chest.

I don't know who the first stripper ever to do a bucks party was, or how the moves were passed down generation after generation, but there are moves and gags you'll see in almost every show.

Get the buck on a chair in the middle of the room and give him a lap dance. Push your titties in his face, flip your hair around to 'Sweet Cherry Pie' by Warrant (I blame the sex industry for my love of 80s hair metal now).

First off—the skirt, then the bra and lastly, as you fire up the room with hand gestures and suggestive winks—the G-string. But always a G-string with clips on the side—you want one swift movement, not a fumble with your drawers like you're in a changing room.

You've got the 'strawberries and cream'—lie on your back with your pussy out and shake a can of whipped cream with a seductive look on your face. Squirt it right above the top of your pussy, place an Allen's lolly on top and crook your finger towards the buck. The gag is that when he goes for it, you snap your legs up and hold his head in a vice-like grip. Eventually, when I started doing shows, I'd sometimes put the whipped cream on my asshole. I guess because I'm a fucking psychopath.

Another brilliant gag—take a Chupa Chup, suck it and roll it around in your mouth and then with a smile on your face, put it up your cunt. Roll it around in there, pull it out and pop it in a dude's mouth. Watch as everyone freaks out.

Other great time-killers for a fifteen-minute show include slathering yourself in baby oil and rolling over the buck, pouring oil over your ass and shaking it to the sound of 'Here I Go Again' by Whitesnake. When you're thoroughly covered in carpet hairs, baby oil, men's aftershave and the sweat from the guy you've just been writhing all over, get into the paddling pool. I like the clamshell ones

I had as a kid. They're very Birth of Venus. The paddling pool is great because rather than have a shower, you just soap up your back and crack in front of all the guys.

There would always be one guy at every bucks party strip show, without fail, who wanted to act out some homoerotic fantasy on his friend. He'd step forward from the crowd, and, unclasping his belt, turn to you and say, 'Whip him.' Not my thing. But seeing a market for closeted BDSM kinksters, I did eventually offer a dominatrix show where I'd bridle the buck and ride around on him naked.

I was so impressed by the strip shows, but this was also the point at which I realised that the men had less respect for you the further you were willing to go. As the show would start, I'd be sitting front and centre with the guys. Usually, at some point, one of them would turn to me and make a comment. It could be about the shape of the stripper's pussy, or that the Chupa Chup trick was gross, or that 'the show's fun and all, but I'm glad you don't do them.' I could sense that some of the girls I worked with felt superior too, seduced by this distinction of 'good whore' and 'bad whore'. Sure, they had their tits out, but at least they weren't spreading their asshole in the middle of the room. As an eighteen year old who wanted approval and acceptance, I initially fell for this, but quickly realised it was the men and their slut-measuring system that were the fucking problem.

At this point in my life, I was also very ignorant about drugs. I smoked pot, I drank alcohol and I'd taken a No-Doz but I'd never experimented with anything harder. I had a vague understanding that cocaine was something people did but I had no interest in trying it, preferring to smoke a spliff with the one weird stoner guy at the party. Once again, 'good whore' and 'bad whore' came into play as the men congratulated me for not doing a line of coke, and making fun of the girls who had, all while wiping white residue off their own noses.

Maybe, I thought to myself, *men are a bit fucked*.

My lack of street savvy about drugs came into play when I went on a job to Shepparton with another girl I didn't know very well. Well, I did know her, and I was terrified of her. We had done a job together a few weeks back for a group of coked-up . . . well, cunts. Natalia was tanned with huge fake tits, and the guys loved her. She went into the bedroom and came back out in just a G-string. The guys turned to me and asked if I would take my clothes off too.

'Sure,' I said. 'For fifty bucks.'

When I wouldn't budge on getting half naked for free, they turned on me. Guys turning on you at a job was the absolute seventh circle of hell. They'd paid for you to be there, they wanted their money's worth and if you didn't jump when they said jump, they'd make you out to be the worst whore of all—the party-killer whore. The men at that party called me ugly, laughed at my body, ignored me when I asked them if they wanted a drink and pulled out their biggest, baddest move—using any opportunity they could to highlight how great Natalia was. Eventually I snapped, called the ringleader a 'fucking dipshit,' picked up my bag and went to the bathroom to cry. Natalia came in, teetering on her 8-inch heels.

'Don't cry,' she said to me half-heartedly, counting her fifties. 'It'll let them know they've won.'

We had a four-hour drive there and back. It was getting dark on the ride home and we decided to stop at this dinky little roadhouse pub for parmas and chips. At this point I'd softened towards Natalia, who I'd figured out as just a hardened veteran stripper, not someone inherently spiteful or nasty. Natalia knocks back another Jack and Coke, I finish my wine and we drunkenly walk out to the car.

'Fuck,' says Natalia, looking around her car. 'I can't find my glasses.'

'How badly do you need them?'

'I can't see very well without them, but we'll manage. You'll just have to tell me what speed I'm going at.'

Great. I'm driving home with a drunk, legally blind stripper in the middle of the night and I'm apparently her guide dog.

We speed off down the highway and I keep one beady eye on the odometer.

'I think it's 100 here,' I say, looking at the dashboard with the needle quivering at 120 km/h.

'I need to have a pipe to straighten up. I'm just going to pull over.'

At this point, I'm completely mystified. A pipe? I wonder where Natalia has hidden a bong, and how she plans on smoking a cone in the middle of the freeway, or how she plans on packing said cone when she can't see glowing neon lights on her dashboard.

Natalia is rustling around the back seat and pulls out this totally bizarre-looking glass thing and I'm all like, oh, it's one of those portable weed-smoking things I've seen at the smoke shop.

She gets out a lighter and a tiny little baggie. Inside is what looks like shards of glass.

'Look out for any cops,' she says to me, ducking behind the backseat and smoking what I understand now, with years of wisdom behind me, is meth.

I roll down the window and stick my head out like a panicked golden retriever, because I'm freaking out that this mystery smoke is going to hotbox me.

'Shut the window!' she hisses at me.

The first time I ever did harder drugs, I ended up giving a guy a hand job for $200. I did a line in this beautiful house by the beach, all architectural angles and floating staircases. I felt really fucking good. I wandered around, smoking cigarettes and chatting, and then I felt it—the cocaine shits. I searched frantically for an empty bathroom as my asshole rumbled and shook. The bathroom I took my first drug-fuelled poop in was attached to a bedroom, and as I walked out, I found an equally high man lying by himself on the bed.

'Come over here,' he said, patting the empty space next to him.

I lay down and began to chat, but he stopped me.

'How much for you to give me a hand job?'

It was then that I noticed the box of tissues and container of moisturiser by the bed. To this day, I look back and wonder, was this the jack off room? Was this man some kind of hand job fetishist who bought said tools for jacking off with him?

Because I was high and horny, I thought to myself, why not.

'$200.'

He gave me the cash, flopped out his dick and it took me all of about three minutes to make him come. I washed my hands and left the room silently, unsure exactly how I felt about what happened. It wasn't the jacking off that scared me, but the reaction I would get if my work friends found out. I had transgressed the unspoken agreement that we were not hookers and as much as I liked my friends, I knew they would disapprove of me for what I did.

Mulling this over and also regretting not giving my hands a secondary rinsing, I walked down the stairs to find Elle and Olivia pacing outside a bedroom door. I walked closer and could see there was a hotel slipper wedged underneath. They were pushing at the door, trying to unjam it. We could hear muffled sounds coming from inside. I looked at Elle and Olivia and I could see the panic on their faces.

We began to bang on the door, demanding they open it. Eventually, some of the guys heard the commotion and they forced the door open with their shoulders. Inside, the room was pitch black and there were two guys in the bed. They sprang up and quickly got dressed, throwing their clothes on. I recognised one of them as the buck. In the bed was one of the waitresses. She was crying. We helped her out; she had Bambi legs from drinking. In that moment I felt intensely afraid. Whatever had happened in that room, we were not supposed to get in and help her. We weren't always going to be safe.

Baby hooker

I have two vivid memories from a girl-on-girl orgy shoot I did.

When it wrapped up, a group of us went down to the beach for a swim. It was empty except for one lonely figure on the horizon, throwing branches into the ocean for the dog to catch. Slowly we began to undress, wading into the sea, feeling the sun beat down on our bare backs and chests, the waves sweeping over our naked bodies. Our bikini bottoms were tossed onto the sand. Daphne, the director, picked them up as she turned her camera on (of course, god forbid a moment of actual joy went uncaptured and unsold). We were all oblivious to the blinking red light as we splashed each other in the sea. This time, it wasn't for show. There was a raw, earthy sensuality to our decision to go naked in the ocean, one I believe that fucking on camera gave us permission to do. We had stepped so far outside of the norm that we could see norms for what they are—restrictive, stifling. Why did we need clothes to swim in? I lay on my back in the water and gazed up at the sky. Again, I felt I had found my people.

The second thing I remember is a girl from the group telling me about working in a brothel. I didn't know what a brothel was. She said to me, we have TVs in the rooms we can watch when we don't have any clients. She said, we keep the same room all day. In my mind I saw a room with purple walls and faded carpet, a tiny and ancient television perched on a dusty side table. It played daytime talk shows. I saw faded curtains, a grimy window that looked out on to a suburban street.

Could I do that? I didn't know. Escorting seemed safer somehow. More private. I was of course an idiot who had no clue but, in my mind, somehow being in hotel rooms with strangers seemed the safer option.

I decided to go with the agency whose website I liked best. It said they specialised in young girls and as I looked at the photos of smooth, taut bodies and glossy hair, I decided I wanted in. I wanted to be one of those beautiful girls, with their perfect tans and smooth, anonymous faces. When I saw the page with the rates on it, I wanted in even more. *A month*, I said, *just while stripping is quiet. That's enough to get me set up.*

I sent in my photos, choosing carefully. Me smiling at the camera, me on set with Daphne in a tight little dress, me with my hands cocked on my hips in my best dress and a pair of glittering earrings. My phone lights up an hour later and I receive a call from Stacey, the owner. She wants me to come to Sydney that week. They will cover my flights and accommodation and take it out of my commissions. Alex, the other owner, will pick me up from the airport. I send a photo of my passport to confirm I'm over eighteen and my legal name for the flight ticket, and I'm booked in. They'll even shoot photos of me for the website, they say. They promise me I'm sure to be busy as a new girl. What they mean is *you are eighteen and you have never had sex for money before. You are about to make a lot of money.*

When I tell Peter of my plan he says, 'Just—please be safe.'

Alex picks me up from Sydney airport in a black Mercedes convertible. It's a two-seater and we have to squeeze my suitcase in the back. Alex is handsome and charming, and dressed in Adidas tracksuit pants with a gleaming gold watch on his hand. He drives me to the hotel in Potts Point, chatting all the way.

'Our clients are great,' he says as he turns a corner, one hand on the steering wheel. 'Really nice guys. They see a lot of our girls. It's best to be nice to all of them, because they tend to book again and again. You'll learn how to do that in this industry, how to make them want to come back. Some of my girls don't even need to see new guys. It's funny, you'll say to them—oh, Carl made a booking for tonight, and they'll say, oh great! You really start to look forward to seeing your clients.'

When we get to the hotel, they ask for a credit card for a bond for the room.

'I don't have one,' I say.

Alex pulls out a black American Express card.

'Don't worry about it.'

I've only ever been in an expensive hotel room once before. For my eighteenth birthday my sister got me a room at The Hilton, and my friends and I smuggled my bong and a bottle of vodka in. We smoked weed on the plush bed and did shots in the bathroom.

This was different. This was my workroom.

Alex pulls out a box of condoms.

'Right. I'll give you a box now, but you'll need to go and buy more, and lube as well. Before the booking, take a condom and unwrap it, and place it under the pillow. That means when you go to . . . do the booking, it will be right there. You won't have to fumble around for it.'

He unwraps a condom and shows me how to place it under the pillow, thankfully, as I'm sure I couldn't have figured that out on my own. He keeps talking as he walks around the room, and I feel like I should be taking notes.

'Ask them to have a shower first but always give them a kiss when they walk in. Text me when they arrive, when you get the money and when they leave. If I don't hear from you, I'll knock on the door, and if you don't answer I'll kick the door in. When they kiss you, don't pull away. It makes it obvious you aren't into it. Count the cash and put it away somewhere safe. I'll come and collect the commissions from you at the end of the weekend. Most girls will separate the money and put it straight into an envelope. Some of our guys pay on credit card, so we will transfer that money to you. Text me your bank details. Remember, these guys like that you are young and pretty, so don't overdo it with the make-up. Don't wear perfume, you'll leave a scent on them.'

He spots the packet of Marlboro Lights and my lighter in my handbag.

'Make sure you brush your teeth after, OK?'

With that, he gives the room a final look and claps me on the shoulder.

'Don't worry, you'll do great.'

My first booking is a wheezing, arthritic, seventy-year-old man. He has booked me for three hours. He arrives with a bottle of champagne and when I open the door, he leans in and kisses me square on the mouth. I can feel his dry lips and scratching tongue poking around. I use my free hand to grab the bottle and usher him in. I pour half of it into one wine glass and give him a splash in another. I hide the bottle in the fridge for later. I knock back my entire glass. As he emerges from the shower, I take a deep breath and smile as I lead him over to the bed.

'You are very pretty,' he says. His skin is translucent and looks like it's hanging on by a thread. A stiff breeze and he'd be gone. He reaches up to my face and touches it, looking into my eyes. 'Yes, and very . . . young.'

I start to undress but he stops me.

'Come lie next to me and tell me some stories.'

'What kind?' I say.

'Well,' he says, running his hands up my legs, 'tell me about high school. Did you kiss any boys? Do anything naughty?'

He comes towards me, spit bubbling at his lips.

'Open wide,' he says, grasping my face with his hands. Shockingly, dust doesn't fly out of his mouth but instead a big loogie.

'How did it go?' Peter says, picking up after one ring.

'He spat in my mouth!'

'What!'

'This seventy year old spat in my mouth!'

'Rank!'

I don't remember much about the next bookings. They all seemed like the same man, somebody in a hurry with an hour to spare. Business suits, bland, nothing noteworthy. If this was what escorting was, I felt like I could deal with it.

As a client left and I was putting aside Alex's money, I could feel a wetness between my legs. I reached down, then brought my fingers up. Bright red blood.

I remembered the conversation I'd had with the girl from the shoot about working in a brothel, I had her number in my phone, she'd given it to me before we'd left.

'I'm in Sydney with an escort agency, I've just got my period and I don't know what to do. I have another booking tonight. Can I use a tampon? Will they feel it?' I get this out in one breath, pacing my apartment balcony, chain-smoking.

I walk to the chemist down the street and find the sea sponges. I buy several. I take them back to the hotel, boil the kettle and place one of the sponges inside a coffee mug. I pour boiling water over it ('To sterilise it,' she said) and wait for it to float to the top. Then I squeeze the water out and push it inside of me like a tampon. Easy. It feels just like your cervix to a condom-covered dick, apparently.

My next client is fucking me hard in doggy style on the bed. He's relentless, pushing his whole body weight into mine. I feel myself clenching on to the sponge, hoping to dear god it stays up there. He's panting and moaning, his hands clenched on my hips and then I feel him freeze. He starts yelling and I look behind me.

I'm a heavy bleeder. In high school, I sneezed in the middle of history class and blood shot out of me and my pad and sprayed all over the green-checked cotton skirt of my school uniform. How's that for a story about Year 10?

It looks like a murder scene. My period is splashed all over the white sheets, soaking through to the mattress. It covers the condom, his legs have red smeared across them. He starts screaming.

I can't move or speak. I watch as he hobbles to the shower, stark naked, his hands covered in blood. The water turns on and I see the steam rise quickly as he runs the scalding water. He's scrubbing frantically with the hotel soap; the suds are turning baby pink. I don't say anything when he starts berating me about working on my period. Okay, you weird fucking man-child. I'm staring at the blood splatters over the bed, fixated on them. When the door slams I finally look up and I can't help myself. I start hysterically laughing, and the sheer force of my giggles propels the sponge out of me with a sad plop onto the bed.

Alex doesn't find it funny at all. The client has called up to complain, and he knocks on my door an hour later. I am treated to a step-by-step instruction from Alex about how to work on my period, and having this hot man give me a sex ed lesson makes me want to roll myself inside a giant maxi pad and stay there forever.

My last client is nice. He doesn't force his tongue down my throat when he walks in the door. He carefully takes off his suit jacket and hangs it in the cupboard. We make out on the bed, rolling around. He presses himself on top of me, rubs my pussy through my Playboy underwear. I am surprised to find that I'm wet. When he leans in to kiss me, I don't have to force my head. That's the thing about whoring. It's not about how they look, it's how they touch you, talk to you, make you feel. He wasn't an attractive man, but he knew how to pace himself, knew how to make me laugh. The chemistry was there and when he came, he rolled over and tucked me into his chest, where I lay and stroked his stomach.

'I hope you don't mind, but I smoke,' he says.

'I do too.'

He looks at me, and then looks outside.

'I think I might stay another hour.' He takes out his wallet to pay the difference.

I take the fifties and put them aside. This time I don't give Alex his cut. I got this one all on my own.

The world's worst porn star

Daniel has taped up my nipples.

I'm standing naked in the backyard, my arms out to the side and my feet spread apart. He shakes the can and with careful aim, sprays tan down my back and over my legs.

'Thigh out!'

I oblige.

My nipples are taped up because Daniel is, in his own words, 'so gay that he finds female nipples confronting'. I feel that this is a small price to pay for getting my tan even and streak free. Tomorrow I shoot my first big-budget adult film.

Daniel and I spent the whole day drinking white wine and watching *Sailor Moon*, and bleaching the black dye from my hair. Finally, Daniel tapes 24-inch extensions into my hair and finishes it off with a blow dry. I am now a redhead.

I had left my apartment on Smith St and moved to St Kilda, into one of the spare bedrooms of the house Daniel and his boyfriend owned. Another housemate, Sarah, lived in the other room down the hall. The four of us ate dinner together every night, cleaned the house together, played with one of Daniel's many cats or took turns walking the dog he had rescued from a puppy farm. A year of coming home to an empty house when I returned from a shoot or a topless gig had weighed on my shoulders. Here I would come home and hear the sound of the TV in the front room, see the light under Sarah's door. We fell into a domestic rhythm quickly and with ease.

Daniel had initially baulked at my choice of career, but with time he had come around. 'What's your porn star name going to be? Have you picked one yet?' he asked me, as I lifted my hands above my head so he could tan my stomach.

'I'm not sure.'

I had a name I used with Daphne, but it didn't feel glamorous enough for a proper film.

We go inside and Daniel pulls out some butcher's paper and markers. We sit at the kitchen bench and write down various names, playing with spelling and swapping words around. He writes my name down and moves the letters about.

'Tira!'

We start to laugh but the more we say it, the more we begin to like it, and so begins another identity for me.

Daniel helps me pack that night. We go through the script sent by the director, Director X, outlining my scenes. Director X has placed references for outfits—swimwear, dinner party, casual, marked next to the name of the scene, *Boy/Girl, Girl/Girl, Double Blow Job.*

When I arrive at the shuttle bus the next morning, armed with a suitcase and a packed lunch from Daniel, Director X looks me up and down.

'What have you done to yourself?'

He's staring at my hands and knees, where my dry skin has soaked up every drop of fake tan. In the light of the house, I looked sun-kissed. In the 9 a.m. sunlight, I am electric orange.

Director X and I are off to a bad start.

The other actors are milling about. There's a girl a few years older than me; a tall, bookish-looking man with glasses is carrying her pink luggage. A muscly Italian man wearing sunglasses is drinking out of his water bottle, looking nervous. I spot the crew, easy to tell by the huge camera bags they are lugging along with them. Down by the entrance to the bus is a woman with brown hair who's laughing and smoking, talking to another muscular guy with a shaved head. They see me and wave me over.

'Is this your first time shooting with Director X?' says the man, with a heavy English accent.

'Yes! I've worked with Daphne before.'

'I'm Matthew.'

'I'm Elise,' says the woman, shaking my hand. 'I'm writing a story for *Penthouse* magazine.'

I smile and greet them, and as we chat I see in my periphery a man clad in a black turtleneck and leather pants, with black aviator sunglasses—on a thirty-five degree day. Director X is speaking to him, and pointing at me, and the man in black lowers his sunglasses to look at me. He strides over.

'Hello,' he says in a thick German accent. 'I'm Claus and I'm doing the hair and make-up. That fake tan is very bad, yes? We will scrub it off when we get to the location.'

Matthew claps me on the shoulder.

'I don't think it looks that bad,' he says, smiling at me. 'Let's all get on the bus now, shall we? This is going to be so fun.'

On the bus I can feel my nerves begin to kick in. I feel like a complete amateur surrounded by these people, most of whom have performed many times before. We stop at a petrol station and cafe, and everyone gets out to buy their lunch. I was used to making money, but I had also become very good at spending it. I was down to my last $50. Eating my home-packed lunch and hiding my lunch bag next to me, I watch the rest of the crew pay for coffees and sandwiches.

Director X has booked out an entire campsite to shoot his porno on. Set on sprawling acres of grey and blue gum trees, the campsite sits in a semicircle around paddocks full of glossy brown cows. There is a lake, complete with a jetty and a small lodge. Director X points this out as the perfect spot for the double blow job. We are staying in dormitory-style rooms with bunk beds, and we have a mess hall and a unisex shower block. Elise, smiling, asks if she can share a room with me. I am glad for her company. It's starting to feel more like a school camp than a party of perverts.

I've barely opened my suitcase when Director X knocks on the door.

'We are going to start shooting in an hour. You've read your script, right?'

'Yes, I have.'

Daniel and I had stood in the kitchen, telling each other to 'touch me there' and 'fuck me like you mean it!' and dramatically pausing.

Director X hands me a bottle of exfoliant and looks at it pointedly.

'Forgot to tell you. No fucking off camera here.'

———

I'm standing in the shower block, frantically scrubbing at my tan. It's not budging.

Oh well.

I walk to the sinks and find Matthew brushing his teeth. Stark naked. I clutch my towel to myself and look away.

'Sorry!' he says, spitting the foam into the sink. 'But we're all going to be naked soon, anyway? I thought, what's the big deal?'

He grins at me, rinses his mouth and walks out, giving me a gentle slap on the ass.

———

I'm walking down the hill in cut-offs and cowboy boots because I feel this is appropriate porn set attire. Everyone has gone ahead to start shooting the first blow job scene, but I don't need a map to work out where they are. I follow the moaning sounds and turn a corner to find the brunette girl from the bus jacking off Matthew next to some kind of post-modern sculpture. Elise sees me and puts a finger to her lips—we are rolling. Brown-haired girl is called Destiny and, as I soon find out from Elise, the bookish-looking guy holding a reflector to bounce the light off her pussy is her husband, Mitch. Mitch looks on casually as Destiny gags on Matthew's huge dick, mascara running down her face. He's face fucking her, her knees are picking up the red dust from the ground and I'm standing there thinking, *is it too late for me to try to hitchhike back to Melbourne?*

Claus has spotted me. He's striding towards me clutching a hairbrush, as though he can read my mind.

'Let's get you ready,' he says, the heat making his frizzy hair stand on end.

Claus paints my face and straightens my hair. He's done the Jenna Jameson porno look—the latte-coloured lipliner and nude pink lip, a heavy contour and false lashes. It's my solo masturbation scene. I am going to get my cunt out in front of Claus, Mitch, Director X, Elise and the entire crew and diddle myself on a swing and try to make it look glamorous and sexy. I'm wearing a tiny black Lycra dress, no panties and 7-inch heels. I saunter towards the tyre swing, hoof one leg in the air and straddle it like a bucking bronco. Then my shoe slips and I fall ass over tit into the dirt.

'Cut,' says Director X.

We try again, and again. Each time I do something wrong. I block the camera; I miss my lines. I am becoming more and more flustered. I do not enjoy having people watch me and I feel small and uncomfortable under Director X's increasingly pissed off face. Eventually Michael Bay over here relents and lets me finish myself off on the grass, like any normal person would, rather than violently masturbating over play equipment like a sex predator.

Cool, I think, *just got to do that six more times.*

Claus and I are in the back of the jeep. It's bumping up what appears to be a cliff face, and we have to duck to avoid being hit by branches. It's late afternoon and the sun has faded to a soft, golden light. My hair is swept back in a high ponytail, and I'm wearing my best dress—a shimmery, golden-flecked mini-dress with long billowing sleeves and a plunging V-neck. Daniel and I found it at the op shop in Fitzroy. Across from me sits Elise, notebook in hand. Matthew and the crew are riding in the jeep ahead of us. I'm jiggling my foot in anticipation.

I have to admit, Matthew is good looking. His head shaved, his body built and muscular, and the accent . . . I learn that the roughness in his voice comes from South London, and when he says my name, I like it. He makes everyone on the crew laugh, the energy coming from him is big and warm.

We reach the peak of the hill and come to a clearing. Positioned high, we can see over the gullies and ranges of the mountains surrounding the lodge. The campsite looks tiny from up here. The wind whips through the gum trees and the sun has begun its slow descent.

'We need to move quickly to catch the light,' says Director X, breaking me from my trance.

The crew set up, and I stand over by one of the rocks. It's smooth and flat, like a bed. Matthew stands beside me and we wait side by side.

He leans into my shoulder and says in my ear so nobody can hear, 'I'm looking forward to fucking you.'

'Action,' says Director X.

———

I went back to try and find the scene, but it was hidden behind a paywall and I was a cheapskate. I wanted to see if it looked the way it felt. I remember Matthew and I leaning in to kiss each other and his hand gripping my hair. It felt different to all the other scenes I had shot. It felt how it felt when I was in my own bedroom, touching somebody who was there, present with me. I didn't need to fake the moan when Matthew touched me, grabbed my ass, pressed his hands into my waist to position me. We knew we had to move into the next position, start the blow job scene, but we couldn't stop making out with each other. I forgot the crew was there and lost myself with him. I didn't care about whether I was blocking the shot, I just wanted him inside me. I kicked off my underwear, went into doggy on the rock and pushed Matthew's cock inside me. I remember he had to pause at times, trying to stop himself from coming too early. He had his hand around my throat, his mouth to my ear.

'This is too romantic!' says Director X.

The next day I worked out why Director X didn't like me. It was something I could sense about him, the way he looked at me and spoke to me with a sharpness he didn't have for the other cast members.

Destiny and I are shooting a girl-on-girl scene down by the lake. Destiny knew what she was doing. She knew how to suck dick on camera, she knew how to contort her body and to get the up-close, dick-entering-pussy shot. Mitch, her ever-present shadow, would film her and help direct content. As I walked down the hill to the lake, I could see her and Director X laughing and talking.

'Do you have any other bikinis?' Director X says to me.

I look down at the one I'm wearing. It's a simple black bikini. Destiny is in a blue one.

'This is all I brought.'

Director X rolls his eyes at me.

'Destiny, do you have one she can borrow?'

I look over at Destiny. We are the same height, but she's about four sizes smaller than me. I'm a full DD cup, she's flat-chested. There's no way I would fit into something she owns.

I look at Destiny, and then over at Director X's wife, who is our camp cook and general house mother. She's helping with the lighting rig. Director X's wife is petite and cute, with the same lean lines to her body that Destiny has. Suddenly it becomes clear to me.

Oh, I think, *I get it now. Director X doesn't want to fuck me.*

I feel myself getting flushed, knowing the shit show that awaits when I try to squeeze my giant tits into one of Destiny's itty bitty bikinis.

Mitch, who I don't think I've heard say one word so far, pipes up.

'I think we have one in there that will work.'

'Go,' says Director X.

I walk silently beside Mitch. We enter their cabin and Mitch digs through the sparkly and bedazzled bikinis in the suitcase, pulling out an Australian flag one.

'This one is big on Destiny.'

I smile at him with gratitude and he smiles back.

I change, walk back and we start shooting. The bikini just covers my cooch and now that I understand what

Director X likes, I feel like a whale next to Destiny. We make out on the grass, spraying each other with the hose. I miss my lines.

Director X cuts and strides over to me.

His voice is low and firm, and his eyes are cold.

'I expect more from you. Let's take a break.'

I can feel the tears start to well up in my eyes and I nod, turning my head away. I don't make eye contact with Destiny or Mitch but walk directly towards Claus in the distance where he's cleaning his make-up brushes. Claus is gay and seems like the safest person there, and, in that moment, he served as a stand-in for who I really needed—Peter.

The tears are streaming from my eyes now and when he looks up at me, I start sobbing.

'Oh, honey,' he says, in his thick German accent. 'Don't you cry, you'll ruin all your make-up.' I sit down and he begins tapping my forehead with his index finger—'It stops the tears.' He begins to fix up my face. Carefully blotting my mascara, he speaks to me kindly and slowly.

'Darling, you are here to be a star. Fuck Director X, and fuck everyone else. Don't let them see you cry. Use this as an opportunity to show everyone just how wonderful you are! You got this. Now, go and finish your scene.'

I went through my scenes with all the energy I had. I paid attention to the camera blocking, moving my body the way I saw Destiny do it. I focused on the moment, being present with the other person. When Rocky and I were doing a boy/girl scene in the games room, I was spread out over a pool table. He was a tradie by day, and he had stamina. He was finger fucking me over the pool table, pounding me with all the strength in his forearms. I felt my entire body clench and then I squirted—all over the camera guy's feet.

That night we have a bonfire and toast marshmallows. Rocky and Destiny are shooting a scene down in the lake house. Mitch offers to do a run to the local service station and brings me back a pack of cigarettes. When I go to get my wallet out to give him cash, he waves it away.

Looking over at Matthew by the fire, I remember the way he felt when we kissed. I take Elise's notepad and write on it and tear off the sheet, folding it in half. I get up to refill my water bottle and drop the note in Matthew's lap as I go past.

As I sit back down, I watch him open it and read it. He looks up at me and smiles.

When everyone goes to bed later, Elise and I lie in our bunk beds. I keep chatting to her until she goes silent, her tiny snores the only sound I hear. I push open the door quietly. It's pitch black outside, apart from the moon illuminating the trees and the light of the buzzing mosquito lamps. I pad down the veranda and try to remember where the teepees are, stubbing my toe on a log on the way. Hobbling, my eyes adjust to the dark and I can see the white canvas tent.

I slip inside.

Matthew is sitting on his sleeping bag.

'I like the note,' he says. He opens it, but I already know what it says.

Want to fuck?

———

The first scene the next day is by a paddock. Claus and I decide on farmgirl-style plaits, and I'm in my trusty denim cut-offs. Rocky is leaning against the fence post, and I'm on my knees. Sheep bleat and a hot north wind blows across my bare legs. Rocky is hard and I'm blowing him, my face tilted so I don't block the shot. We've been going for a while now and I can see Director X is ready to get the pop shot.

'Okay Rocky,' calls out Director X, 'when you are ready, aim for her face. Guys, make sure you're ready to come in for the close-up.'

Rocky's eyes are closed and his face is straining. He brings his hand down to mine and starts stroking his cock. I bring my face down to his balls and start licking them while stroking the inside of his leg.

Rocky's been having issues coming on cue. Matthew told me this last night in the teepee. Apparently the boy/girl scene with Destiny was a disaster. Rocky wasn't used to being in front of cameras any more than I was, and he started going soft. They had to fake the cum shot with Cetaphil inside Destiny's pussy.

I can sense Rocky becoming more anxious and flustered. He's breathing quicker and he's squeezing his eyes shut, with his head tilted up at the sky. Whatever fantasy he's trying to escape to, it isn't working. His dick deflates.

'Give us five minutes,' I say.

I take Rocky by the hand and walk him back to the cabins. I pull him inside and shut the door.

'Lie down on the bed,' I say.

I crawl on top of Rocky and lean down to kiss him and his hands grab my ass and hoist my shorts high. I start grinding against him as we make out and I feel myself getting wet through the crotch of the denim, pressed against his hard-on. Without the camera, Rocky is a different person. He pulls my shorts off and, using those tradie forearms from heaven, pounds my G-spot again. As soon as I start moaning, Rocky flips me on to my back, pushes my legs above my head and fucks me hard. It isn't the tenderness I experienced with Matthew—this is carnal and animalistic. I may not like fucking on camera, but I do like to fuck and having this huge Italian tradie pin me down on the bed and fuck me sideways was exactly what I needed. I'm getting close to coming and my pussy muscles squeeze down on Rocky's dick. He widens his eyes and quickly pulls out.

'Quick!' he says, grabbing my hand. We barrel out the door of the cabin and race down to the field we are shooting in. I barely have time to put my shorts back on (for continuity's sake) before Rocky grabs me by the plaits, holds my head back and blows all over my face. We got the pop shot. That afternoon I go into full porn-star-on-set mode and start strolling around stark naked in my cowboy boots. As I looked around at Claus, Elise, Matthew, Destiny, Mitch, Rocky and the crew eating BBQ around the picnic table, I felt a little sad to be leaving that afternoon. I had bonded with these people over the last 48 hours. The mood had shifted from a bunch of strangers thrown together to feeling like a family. Well, perhaps one of those cult families where nobody's related and they all have sex with each other. Sex work creates a higher level of intimacy between colleagues than in any other industry, in my experience. Perhaps it's the nakedness and consequent vulnerability—both physical and emotional—that any shoot or booking involves. There is a profound kinship and sense of belonging, a rare and valued feeling when you're used to being the outlier.

On the bus ride home, Matthew and I sit next to each other. It's a four-hour journey back but the time goes past quickly. We sit and talk in low voices, not wanting to draw attention to ourselves. We talk about our families and experiences growing up, our sex work, our lives. Eventually, we both fall asleep, curled up next to each other, our hands in each other's laps. I am richer after being paid out by Director X, and I am content.

I arrive home to Daniel's house. I drop my suitcases and handbag in my room, and I rush out to greet everyone. After I've showered and changed, Daniel cracks open a bottle of wine and starts pouring glasses. As we talk about what we feel like for dinner, I exclaim that it's my shout tonight and rush to my room to get my wallet. I search through my bag, a cold panic sweeping over my chest. My wallet isn't in my bag. I know I had it, because I bought cigarettes and a juice at the service station on the return journey. I tear through my suitcase, every pocket of every jacket, trace my steps from the front door to the bedroom. I can't even cry. That was the most money I'd ever had in my life, and it was gone.

The next morning, I lie in the backyard, staring up at the sun, chain-smoking. I hear Sarah and Daniel exclaim over her bags of new clothes and make-up as I contemplate how broke I am. But I couldn't allow myself to string the two together. Maybe it was a coincidence that last night my wallet full of money went missing and this morning Sarah has a whole new wardrobe. I recall the conversation I'd had with her in the kitchen before I left.

'Are you excited?' she said, stirring her coffee. She had done porn too, but never a feature film like this.

'Sort of. I'm nervous. I find it hard sometimes. You know, fucking in front of people. It's hard.'

———

Maybe I was just drunk with lust and dopamine from holding Matthew's hand, and I left a wallet full of cash in it at a service station. Maybe my friend jacked my wallet, the wallet full of money I'd shot twelve scenes for, my payment for my pussy to be out there on the internet for the rest of my days on this earth.

Blue eyes

Josh and I took a bunch of mystery pills and wound up in the dollar store. We are trawling through buckets of paper and plastic flowers, feeling their silky leaves between our fingers. He finds these ropes of vine leaves and tropical flowers, and we walk home, bags bursting with colours. We string them from the ceiling so they hang down the walls, turning the living room into a psychedelic jungle. The shelves are filling with our trinkets—postcards, monogrammed designer tags, crystals and tarot card decks. We found a six-seater corner sofa on the side of the road and lugged it home and covered it with black sheets and faux fur blankets. I don't know exactly when it was that Josh moved in, but he's here every day now. The door revolves with strangers and acquaintances coming over to party.

My phone beeps intermittently between snorting, smoking and hanging with Josh. I hang my work dress on the washing line to try and rid the smell of tobacco and pot smoke from its fibres. I go wherever the agency sends me. The men and the sex and the money rolls through me and I wake up every day and do it all over again. I drift between my home in Brunswick West and hotel foyers. I don't know how to behave yet so when I get into the hotel room, I make a beeline for the minibar and greet them while searching for a bottle of wine. 'Can I smoke in here?' I ask, striking the hotel matchbook before they have a chance to reply. In the bottom of my purse are condoms and matchbooks and hair ties.

Some traumas are buried so deep inside of us that we can't even move when we think about them. We go back to what it felt like when it was happening, our limbs locked, frozen in time. When I was writing this chapter, I would sit down and place my fingers on the keys of my laptop and urge them to move. They wouldn't. I would get up, I'd drink a glass of wine, take a Valium. I'd clean the kitchen, I'd dust the shelves, walk upstairs and splash cold water on my face. Yet I couldn't do it, I couldn't stand the feeling of my words being pushed down and my throat closing over just as I'd felt then. I didn't want to go back there.

When it happened, the only person I told was Josh.

He was my first regular. I would call him Nick. He found me through my agency.

He opened the door and I looked into the room. It was so beautiful, a huge penthouse suite. Nick smiled at me but it didn't quite reach his eyes. They were a shade of light blue that looked like ice where the iris met the pupil.

I really liked the receptionist who sent me the job via text. We used to chat late at night when I was up waiting for work to come in. She texted me saying, this client says he wants to be able to spank you. I said, sure.

Nick leads me into the room, where a bottle of Dom Perignon sits in an ice bucket. Next to the coffee table and the plush couches is a dining room, complete with a six-seater suite. On top of the lacquered wood of the table lies a collection of BDSM gear. There are paddles, riding crops, clamps, a gag, a hood, cuffs and a spreader bar. There are butt plugs and vibrators and anal beads and a huge bottle of Swiss Navy lubricant.

'Get on your knees,' he says to me, and grabs my face. He clamps his fingers around my nose, pushes his cock into my mouth and pisses down the back of my throat. I claw at his legs but I can't breathe and have no choice but to swallow his pee. I gag but he holds my nose tight, forcing me to swallow. I retch and throw up on the carpet. He tosses a towel at me.

'Clean yourself up,' he says. I wipe orange vomit from the white carpet.

Nick was my first BDSM partner. This is unfortunate. I am angry that he took from me what should have been something I did with someone who could be trusted. I was young and naive, and when I saw all those things on the table I was turned on. I wanted to experiment, I wanted to be submissive, but I didn't know you could do it with somebody who cared about you. I thought what we did was normal.

I thought I could make Nick care about me, and I tried my hardest. I let him dog walk me around the room, I endured him caning the soles of my feet. He suffered from issues with his prostate and had to inject something in his cock to make it hard. After he did this, he would use a pump to make it larger. The pump dragged the blood down to the shaft and it would turn purple. When he forced it into my mouth, I could taste the silicon from the pump. The flavour coated my mouth.

One time, he strung my hands up from the ceiling, somehow. He beat me and lashed me so hard that I screamed. For some reason, I never told him to stop. He said, 'I don't care if I have to beat you black and blue, I'll do whatever it takes to get my cock hard again.' After that session, I stared at myself in the bathroom mirror. My back, legs and ass were covered in blue and purple welts. I put my pants on and walked out, wincing as the denim met my raw flesh.

At this point in my life I was cutting myself frequently. When I became overwhelmed I could only withstand the pain if I turned it into something physical. I would sit in my bathroom with a BIC Lady and cut it open, take a single blade out. I'd run it in neat, parallel lines along the inside of my arm or on the side of my legs. I'd watch as blood bubbled out and dripped down my legs and onto the bathroom tiles. That's when I would start crying, at the absurdity of the way I felt and also with relief, as whatever was sitting on my chest was released. I would rock myself back and forth and sob, and then I'd get into the shower and feel the burning from the hot water over the open cuts. I'd put Dettol on and bandage them with gauze and I'd feel healed.

For my next session with Nick my entire inner forearm was a bloody mark and the complete left side of my leg was butchered. I didn't bother to hide them because some small part of me had hoped he would say something. The raw, bloody welts stared back at him as he flogged me. They were there when I had the weights placed on my nipples and the chain between my teeth, him slapping me if I didn't keep my posture straight. He didn't say a word.

I never knew what I would walk into. Sometimes he'd be kinder to me, would let me use my safe word without getting frustrated by me. The next session I'd be punished for that. As soon as he came, he'd go from this cold-eyed sociopath to this clapping his hands on his thighs, chilled-out kinda guy. He'd hand me my money, and then it would be 'a little extra'. The extra could be anything from a hundred to a thousand dollars depending on how much he'd fucked me up that day. But I kept coming back for more.

Nick was a form of self-harm for me.

My boyfriend once had to talk to me through the bathroom door, trying to coax me out again. I rocked back and forth, screaming and crying. We were having sex and he'd slapped me across the face. I screamed at him and ran to the bathroom; I'd seen Nick's hands coming towards me, and me unable to move or say anything.

———

The last time I saw Nick, he had me tied up with a hook in my ass which was attached to my ponytail. If I moved it was excruciatingly painful. He called me a *dumb fucking whore*, and a *stupid slut*. At this point I felt broken by him. I didn't feel like a person anymore. I felt like I had failed him, watching him having to inject his cock and pump it up. I heard his phone ring. It was his wife. He looks at me and tells me to *shut the fuck up*. He answers in a normal voice, slapping his hand against the granite of the kitchen counter and laughing. 'Say goodnight to the kids for me,' he says, before hanging up. I look over at him in surprise and he wrenches my head forward; my asshole almost rips.

I get cuffed to the bed. My feet and hands are locked together. I feel my head against the pillow, and I am relieved. Finally, this will be over. He will fuck me and then I can go home. I leave my body and just watch myself from the ceiling. I'm crying silently, I'm so exhausted by this pantomime performance that I know every scene from, except what happened next.

'. . . rape you,' I hear. Before I can process this, I feel him thrust his entire body weight into my backside and slide his un-lubricated cock into my ass. My spine seizes in pain and I almost pass out. My vision goes black and then I'm back in my body feeling every single inch of his cock in my ass. I feel like my entire back and ass is on fire.

'That's right, I'm going to rape you, you fucking whore—' before he can continue, I feel something come over me. White-hot rage.

'Get, the FUCK off me you fucking PSYCHO!'

I start kicking and screaming. I somehow manage to push him off me by whipping my hands that are cuffed and trying to claw at his face. I want to scrape those cold blue eyes out of their sockets. He uncuffs me, ducking from my flailing limbs. I pick up the bottle of lubricant and throw it at him.

I don't remember what he said because all I could hear was the buzzing in my ears. White noise was filling the room. I pick up my things; my dress is on back to front as I pull it over my head. I bring my hand to my asshole and feel it, when I look back there is bright red blood on my fingers.

I get my handbag and I run to the door, but he blocks the exit. He has extra money for me and it's the thickest wad of bright green notes he's ever given me. He stood at the ATM and said, *this will be her rape money.* I snatch it from his hand and push him to the side, slamming the door behind me. As I walk to the lifts, the adrenaline leaves my body and my legs turn to jelly. There is a palm tree potted in a vase and I reach for it, folding into myself on the carpet. I start sobbing. I look up and see myself in the reflection of the gold mirroring on the lift. Like a carnival funhouse mirror, I am distorted and broken. I don't know who to speak to or what to do. I find my phone and I call Josh, and he answers after one ring.

'He raped me,' I say, 'in the ass.' And then I cry harder because I know Josh is the only one who can understand. He's gay.

Josh calms me down with sympathetic noises and I'm sorrys, and then he says, come to this bar in the city. I walk out of The Hilton and go to The Toff in Town. I go to the bathroom and turn my dress around the right way, use toilet paper to wash the mascara off my face. I blow my nose and comb the snaggles from my hair with my fingers, from where Nick pulled it. I go back out to our private booth with a bunch of strangers and Josh, and I take one of those crisp green notes and roll it into a little tube. Somebody hands me a plate and I sniff one long white line, and then another. I can feel the toilet paper in my lace G-string where I made a pad for my ass.

I <3 My job

One of the regulars at the strip club finds my escorting profile, but I don't know it's him until he opens the door.

'Oh!' I say, 'it's you!'

'It's me!' he says. He seems embarrassed and is shy as he leads me into his house. We are practically neighbours, his home only a block from mine.

He comes into the club every shift. He always buys dances but he's soft spoken and gentle and fades into the background. I've never really looked at him up close before, in the daylight. He doesn't have the cap he usually wears and I can see his face properly for the first time.

I don't like pretty boys. I like my men rough around the edges. I like noses that have been broken and chest hair; I like calloused hands and I like them to smell like aftershave and Cussons Imperial Leather soap. I like slightly crooked teeth. I like flannel shirts that smell worn in.

I realise he is strangely handsome, just the way I like them.

The house is warm, the little heater going in the lounge room. On his big L-seater couch are his two greyhounds, curled up against each other. On the coffee table, among the coasters and vintage *Playboys*, sits a scale and a big brown rock.

When we go to his room to fuck, I see he has a pair of handcuffs hanging from a nail above the bed.

'Use them on me,' I say.

I will die on the hill of the dark horse. It's always the quiet ones who are the real freaks. The strip club customer, polite and respectful, who's a big tipper and never asks for your real name. He's the one who's going to gag you, fuck you and make you come twice in a row as he eats your pussy like it's his last meal on earth.

We go back to the couch and I'm in his tracksuit pants and t-shirt, at his insistence. He sees me looking over at the brown rock.

'Do you . . . want to do some?'

He carefully crushes up the pure MDMA and sprinkles it into a cigarette paper, wrapping it like a Hershey's Kiss. We parachute it and sit there, smoking cigarettes and burning incense until it kicks in.

I'm so warm, so comfortable. One of his greyhounds lies on my lap and falls asleep and the other one's head is on my shoulder and the molly is so strong. My eyes roll into the back of my head and we talk about our trauma, our pain, and our happiness, tripping to Black Sabbath's discography. He doesn't touch me, doesn't interrupt me as I talk and talk, just quietly listens. We smoke a big joint as the wave fades and I look at the clock. I've been here for ten hours. It feels like five minutes.

He stuffs some extra cash in my hand as I put on my clothes.

On my twenty-first birthday, I hear a knock on my door. I put down the crack pipe I'm smoking and push past throngs of people to go and answer it. It's my client—he remembered. He hands me a baggie with a rock of MDMA the size of a fifty-cent piece.

He kisses me on the forehead and wishes me happy birthday. I say, *come in* and he looks around and shakes his head. He fades back into the shadows and I get so high that by 6 a.m., I lose my short-term memory.

———

We wake up in our suite at the Shangri-La and have our morning coffee looking out over the bay and skyline of Hong Kong. What struck me most about David's decision to book this particular room was the second bathroom, discreetly tucked off to the side of the living room. I was thankful for that.

I wasn't exactly sure what David was at this point. Not just a sugar daddy, but boyfriend wasn't quite right either. I met David when he booked me as an escort. We cleaned out the minibar, filled the spa bath and David let me smoke cigarettes in the bathtub, tapping my ash into the empty bottle of Veuve on the floor. And he fucked me right.

I remember David was wearing my panty-dropping weakness when we first met—elastic-sided R.M. Williams boots. I think I like it because it's such a sensible man shoe. It's a no bullshit shoe. It's a no-frills-fucking, straight-down-to-business shoe. This guy's not going to make you eat his ass—he's eating yours.

After breakfast, David asks me what I feel like doing, but he's got his hand up my top and another on my ass, so I know what he feels like doing—me. He allows me my strong soy latte, three Marlboro Gold cigarettes, a shower and to brush my teeth while he lies in bed, checking his emails.

'David,' I say, looking up from blowing him in my negligee, about twenty minutes later.

'Hmmmm . . .?'

'I was thinking it might be nice to get my hair done today?'

David looks up at the ceiling as I deep throat him. I've timed my request perfectly—right on cue, he comes in my mouth. I swallow and cuddle up next to him in bed.

'I'm thinking about going darker. What do you think?'

He plays with my hair.

'Oh yeah. I think that would look good. Why don't you go do that and I'll meet up with you afterwards?'

David peels off a stack of notes and presses them into my hand. He looks at them and gives me a handful more.

'Just in case.'

I find a salon tucked away a few blocks from the hotel. Glamorous Hong Kong women sit there, in their cashmere cardigans and pearls, getting their hair set in rollers. Chinese pop music plays softly in the background. I drink green tea while my hair is taken from a messy, streaky blonde to a deep chocolate brown. The hairdresser blow-dries it into big, bouncy curls. I take out my money and pay.

'You'll look nice for your husband now,' he says to me as he rings me up at the till.

Sometimes David and I do that, play husband and wife. He never corrects the hotel concierge when they call me 'Mrs'. He holds my hand in public, draws me close to him. He likes the way we look together. I play pretend too, and I enjoy it. I wonder what it would be like to actually be his wife, to get to take his credit card and buy myself nice things, to not have to worry about money, to fly all over the world. To send my kids to a private school, drive a Range Rover with a huge diamond on my finger and know that all I needed to do to keep him happy was look hot, make him feel good, and make him come.

David always hides my money somewhere in my purse or my suitcase, never puts it in my hands—it's not part of the fantasy.

'What's your real name?' was what he asked me on our second meeting.

I got the message when he bought me some lingerie for me to wear while we were in Hong Kong. It was white, virginal and lacy. Nothing like the black push-up bras and tiny G-strings I regularly paraded around him in. I rummaged through his suitcase and found one of his worn band t-shirts that smelt like him. When he came in the door and found me lounging in it, I saw his dick get hard through his jeans.

'Leave it on,' he said, pushing my cotton panties to the side, ripping the condom foil between his teeth.

David and I go to a seafood restaurant for lunch. We crack open a bottle of champagne and I tie the plastic bib around my neck, cracking open Chinese crab with my bare hands. He smiles at me, taking out his phone. He snaps a photo of me proudly clasping my crab claw. He likes to take photos of me. Mostly when I'm not looking, or when I'm not wearing any make-up in bed, or when we are out together at dinner.

On the trip, I've been avoiding showering with him, because before we left for Hong Kong, I took my BIC Lady, snapped it open and sliced up and down the outside of my thighs. Always high enough up so it couldn't be seen in a short dress, always with enough time in between clients for them to go from red welts to indiscernible pink blotches. They had begun to heal but if you ran your fingers along the sides of my legs you could feel the tiny scabs.

David feels them the night he fucks me in his t-shirt. He pins me down, and pulls up the shirt, dragging me close to the bedside lamp. Under the light, you can see the tidy, parallel rows where I've dragged the blade across my skin.

'I wish you wouldn't do this shit, Rita. It makes me upset.' He touches them lightly and then pulls me into his stomach, wrapping his arms around me.

David has meetings and kisses me as I sleep, leaves coffee for me. 'Meet me up on the rooftop pool of the hotel for lunch later,' he says. I've changed in to a bright blue Agent Provocateur bikini that I had to pay off on layby. The sales-girl was shoving fistful after fistful of beautiful scraps of lace into my hands, and when I saw the price tags, my heart quickened. I was too embarrassed to put them back, so each week I went to David Jones and put another couple of hundred down on the two sets I'd chosen. I've paid them off in time for our trip. David's eyes light up as I stroll past the pool and to his table. 'You are so beautiful,' he says, pulling me into his arms and kissing me.

'What would you like to do this afternoon?' he asks, as I ash my cigarette into the white and gold ashtray on the table.

'Can we go shopping?' I know that Hong Kong, from my research online, doesn't have as high a luxury goods tax as Australia.

He takes me to a marble and white mall, lined with every store and brand I've ever looked at in my dog-eared fashion magazines.

We walk into Phillip Lim, and there it is. The bright blue bag I've stared at online for weeks. I check the price tag. With my savings and what David has given me on the trip, I can get it. I stroke my hands across the leather, the perfect clasp, and the embossed card that dangles from its straps. I'm in love. I pick it up to take to the counter.

'What are you doing?' says David, taking it from my hands. He pulls out his credit card and I watch as the sales assistant wraps it in creamy tissue paper.

'That's a nice present for your wife,' the sales assistant says.

'Yes—it is,' he replies.

———

Each time we see each other, he goes a bit further down the BDSM rabbit hole. He told me he wanted to be more submissive. He's so polite. He never tops from the bottom, I never have to chase after a hard dick because he doesn't know what turns him on besides 'I don't know, you be in control.' He tips, and he arrives every time smelling like Paco Rabanne. He has a huge dick. This time I can sense he wants to ask me something, but he's too shy. I'm blowing him, but he's going soft even while he's touching my lace bra, the elastic of my stay-up stockings. I look at his eyes and to where they are gazing. My high heels and tight little dress lying on the floor.

I test the waters.

'Do you want to try them on?'

He nods.

I help him into my bra, my lace G-string, show him how to roll up the stockings and clip them into the suspender belt. He's standing in the mirror, turning and admiring himself, running his hands along the cups of the bra.

'You look very pretty,' I say.

I go through my wardrobe, handing him dresses to try on. I help him zip up the backs and adjust them for him. We don't fuck, we don't kiss, and when he leaves, he puts his camouflage print t-shirt, his gold watch and his Nikes back on. He looks sad. I tell him to wait. I dig through my underwear drawer and hand him a set I don't wear anymore.

'You have this.'

———

I've just finished my photoshoot. One of my favourite clients organised the hotel room. I sent him a photo of the place I liked, and he booked it for us. It's so beautiful, this corner-side room right on Darling Harbour. Sliding doors open to an enormous freestanding bathtub. The room is white and cream with polished wood and water views. All I can think about is how irritated I am. The photographer has left and my client walks in, with barely five minutes in between. I'm irritated because my stomach is cramping. My period is about to start. I am exhausted, on the back end of a three-week escort tour around Australia. My uterine lining is shedding, and I didn't bring any Naprogesic. I feel sharp and full of edges. Dinner is at a cosy Italian restaurant. I keep getting up to go and smoke out in the rain, my coat pulled around me against the winds whipping into me from the harbour.

I run a bath back in the room and get into the water and remove my lipstick and liner and peel the lashes from my face. He sits next to me and pours me a red wine, and we talk. I look down and the water has turned pink. I'm bleeding into the bath.

'I'm sorry I've been such a moody, ungrateful little bitch,' I say, my swollen period boobs floating in the water.

'I don't mind,' he says, 'I kind of like it. The real you.'

———

A client showed me some pornography when I was a newly minted brothel worker. I remember we were sitting on the purple cotton sheets, after we'd had sex, smoking. The smell of Glade air freshener and cigarette smoke will always remind me of my first years of full-service work. I asked him what kind of porn he watched. I was curious, and it was often a good conversation starter.

'I'll show you,' he says, pulling out his phone.

He flips through videos he has saved and opens one up. It's a blonde girl, wearing white leggings and stripper heels. I lean into the screen, obscuring his view. I'm so fascinated I take the phone out of his hands.

'She looks like *me*!'

I'm shocked. I grew up in the era of Suicide Girls and alt porn, the models were all heavily tattooed and pierced, but they all had a fairly thin or slim body. The models who adorned my Myspace page had the 'box gap' or thigh gap, that appeared over and over again in my Tumblr feed. The only other porn I saw was in the softcore skin mags, where the girls had tight, toned size-six bodies. I thought that was the ideal for men.

The actress in this video was Alexis Texas, known for her big, round bubble butt. She has thick thighs, a small waist and when she walks into a scene her butt jiggles. She has cellulite, like me.

'Is this, like, a fetish?' I stared at the screen as she slithered out of her white leggings, pants *Vogue* magazine forbade me, a pear shape, to ever wear.

My client starts laughing.

'No!' he says, scrolling through his other videos. More women, some with natural boobs like mine, some with big butts, some with a roll around their stomach. They are smiling, confident, happy and, as I soon learn, a large percentage of the male population regularly jerks off to them. My mind was blown. I could make money off my butt.

———

'You two,' says the client, pointing at another girl and me. The receptionist gets us to both come back into the intro room. She's a night-shift girl too, and we always smile and say hello to each other in the change rooms. I don't know her very well, but she's beautiful. Tall like me, with long, thick brown hair. She has thick thighs and always smells good, her nails perfect long nude almond shapes that click when she does her make-up, sweeping bronzer against the hollows of her cheekbones.

We look at each other, and then the client. He is non-descript. He isn't even part of this story. She is.

He books the spa room, a spa she and I won't go in, knowing nobody ever empties it. Hot little soup of old cum and fake tan. We put him in the shower, hand him the towel, pour a capful of Listerine into the little cup and close the door.

'So,' I say, as we go downstairs to get our condom bags and let reception know to set the timer, 'what do you want to do?'

She looks at me with her big dark eyes, long eyelashes and smoky make-up. Not a hair out of place.

'I'm bi,' she says.

'Oh . . . good. So am I.'

When we get into the room, we pounce on each other. Kissing women is so different, so much softer. We run our hands over each other's bodies and undress each other. I can't stop staring at how beautiful she is, how fucking hot she looks naked. I'm grabbing the drop sheet as she pushes my legs above my head and kisses my body, licks inside my leg, brings her mouth to my pussy. Everything is soft and sensual, and we forget we are in the spa room at the brothel, lost in each other. It was the kind of sex that I fantasised about, magical, lesbian, transcendental and otherworldly.

'Ahem.'

We look up. I've got her boobs smothering my face; her fingers are inside me, we are breathing in each other's mouths. Wet pussies and about to come.

The guy is standing there, pasty white, his dick out and hands on his hips.

'You ladies look like you're having a lot of fun there, ha-ha . . . time for me to join in?'

She looks at me and we share a look. Sadness, laughter, *fuck our lives . . .*

'Come here babe,' she says to the guy, reaching out her hand.

He wheezes and pants. 'Oh yeah!' she says, as he fucks her in doggy, his sweat beads dropping onto her back. She looks at me, rolls her eyes. He moves to me, gets me on my back and I kiss his tight lips, his grey stubble. 'I'm . . . gonna . . . come.' He ejaculates limply inside the condom and rolls off me.

She and I wriggle to the side of the bed so we can spoon each other, I breathe in the sugary sweet smell of her perfume and she brings her hands between my thighs.

'You two really got into that,' he says, staring at the ceiling.

'Mmmm,' I say, curled into her. 'We did.'

Brown shower

I'm in my lounge room in Brunswick. My bong is on the coffee table and I'm hanging out with my pot dealer. He has a spinal injury and is mostly bed bound, but sometimes when he gets his Endone script filled he comes over to my place and we watch back-to-back episodes of *Tim and Eric*.

My work phone dings.

I pick it up, reading the text. I read it again, rubbing my eyes. I can't work out if I'm so high that I'm actually in my own episode of *Tim and Eric* right now.

'Jean Paul,* how much money would you charge somebody if they wanted you to take a shit on them?'

* Just like nearly everyone in the book, this is, of course, *not* my pot dealer's real name. I'm not a snitch. And it's also funny to think my pot dealer is a French man in a beret.

'Ah, I don't know. Like, a hundred bucks?'

'What about if they wanted you to suck their dick too?'

'Wait, are you sucking their dick before or after you've shitted on it? That's going to be extra, dude.'

'Damn Jean Paul, you'd suck a dick with your own shit on it?'

This client wants to see me tonight, for an outcall at a hotel in the city. He wants full service, and for the grand finale, he wants me to take a shit on him—or, as it's also known—a brown shower.

I start frantically running around the house, fumbling like a stoner idiot as I try to wrap my mind around this booking.

'Jean Paul, I don't know how the fuck to do this!'

My pot dealer is one step ahead of me. He's started googling 'human toilet'. He holds his iPhone up and shows me the screen. It's a grinning face sandwiched inside the lid of a toilet, mouth slightly agape, hand on a hard dick.

I lose it completely. I'm doubled over, clutching my sides as Jean Paul wipes tears from his eyes.

'Maybe,' he wheezes, 'you can go to Bunnings and get a toilet lid and bring it with you.'

'You have to drive me,' I say, as I pour myself a glass of wine. I have some dexies in my kitchen drawer, and I smash them under my credit card. I grind them into a fine powder, cut a line and snort it. I leave a second line for later.

I open my bathroom cupboard and I find it, the tube of Microlax. I shower, shave, do my make-up and stuff my purse with condoms, baby wipes and the laxative. One last line of dex, a bong hit and I fill my wine glass again. It's a traveller for the road. I grab the bottle too. I'll need it for after.

The atmosphere in the car is tense. I can feel my butthole contract with every jolt over a speed hump, and Jean Paul is taking the back roads so the cops don't pick him up for being very clearly out of his mind.

'Oh my GOD, what the FUCK is that!' I say, clutching my chest.

Jean Paul screeches the car to a halt. Ahead of us we can see flashing lights and an ominous shadowy figure.

Me, being both tweaked and high, hiss, 'It's the cops. Go. Go!'

Jean Paul pulls up out the front of The Great Southern on Spencer Street. The lights flicker 'Grat Suthn'.

'Ah . . . good luck?'

'Thanks. Can you pick me up in an hour?'

'No worries. I'm going to get drive-through.'

I want so badly to get back in the pot smelling fug of Jean Paul's Mitsubishi Lancer, with its carpet of empty energy drink cans and overflowing ashtray, and go chow down on a bucket of fried chicken in a carpark somewhere.

I turn on my heel and trudge into the hotel.

I knock on the door, and a small, bespectacled man appears. I'd love to pretend I expected something else, but stereotypes exist for a reason.

My eyes look like a nocturnal marsupial's and I reek of pot, which I've tried to disguise with this sugary sweet perfume, so I just smell like the brownies my brother makes.

'Uh, hello,' I say, awkwardly shuffling past him into the room.

'Would you like a drink?' he says, sitting on the bed.

I look around for the alcohol but I realise he's pointing to the tap. I think about my bottle of red wine, under the seat in Jean Paul's car.

'I'm good, but thank you.'

I count the cash he gives me and put it in my handbag, next to the tube of butt laxatives.

We sit down on the bed awkwardly, and I take off my dress. He leans in and I pucker up, expecting a kiss, but instead I feel his tongue slurp up and down my face like an enthusiastic golden retriever.

I go to pull away but then something inside me clicks. This guy wants me to shit on him, what was I expecting? Regular foreplay?

I decide to get with his vibe and return the golden retriever face lick. He's ecstatic, and we lick each other's faces for a while. Sometimes, you've just got to go with the flow of the wackiness. If you resist it, you'll want to punt yourself through the nearest pane of glass to the road below. If you just shrug your shoulders and do whatever the weird thing is, it's mostly just funny and a good story.

He pounces on me and paws at my boobs. There's a bit of fumbling, some terrible sex that I give a Meryl Streep-grade performance of enjoying and then, we get to the grand finale.

You know those toilet dreams? Mine is always about me needing to go to the loo and I raise my hand (inexplicably, my fear of shitting is linked to Year 10 maths class). The teacher is like, hey, you need to shit, my dude? There's the toilet, right near the blackboard, where it's always been. Right there, buddy, no door, you just do your thing while I explain Pi to the class.

So, I look up from the bed and the assortment of condoms, dildos and lubes and see the bathroom. The pristine white bathtub, the tiny shower or the toilet bowl. Choose your fighter.

Because I'm not a fucking monster, if somebody wants me to piss or shit on them, I take it to the bathroom where the surfaces are easy to wipe down with a wet hand towel and some baby wipes. Sometimes I'll be in a booking with a client who wants a golden shower, and he'll get himself all comfy on the bed surrounded by absorbent, spongy pillows and duvet and white sheets, and I'm like, are you for real?

I decide on the bathtub. I feel in terms of geometry and space per metre, and using my Year 10 algebra, the shit that will be flying out of me has more space to . . . be.

'The bath is a giant toilet bowl,' I say to myself under my breath.

My client settles himself into the bath, butt naked with a raging boner. He folds his arms over his chest like a mummy in a sarcophagus.

Suddenly, I remembered a word of warning from the dominatrix forum I'd looked at in the car, chain-smoking out the window.

'Whatever you do, keep your eyes CLOSED!' I say.

I realise now that that wasn't going to happen. This dude didn't cough up this chunk of change for a purely physical experience, a solid thud hitting his chest. He wanted the visual element too.

I squeeze the Microlax up my butthole and turn on all the taps in the bathroom. Time slows down, just one long TICK with each second that passes as the laxatives start opening my lower colon. I wiggle my butt in the dude's face, the world's weirdest lap dance. I've got one leg up on the side of the tub, the other on the floor. Suddenly I feel my guts clench and seize up. Time has now changed to race car driver hurtling towards the finish line. The train is leaving the station folks. I take a dump on him.

I look down at my . . . handiwork. This was definitely a different experience to the old toilet bowl peek.

'You kept your eyes open, didn't you?'

He nods at me, his eyes going pink around the retina. They look like a magician's rabbit's already. Should I have gotten him to sign a disclaimer?

He stands up and poop falls off him into the bath. I stand there awkwardly, and then cough and say, 'Want some help with that?'

He shakes his head, takes the detachable showerhead and

begins to clean up. My poop floats down the bath and into the drain, where it gets stuck and he has to push it down.

What struck me most about this was not the absurdity of this man stuffing my shit down a drain, but the look of melancholy that passed over his face while he did it. It wasn't the clean-up job, but the fact that the fantasy had happened for him. This guy getting to watch a woman taking a shit was his wedding day moment, where you look over at the $30,000 you've spent and are like, *is this it?* He did the thing that he thought was the missing piece and he still felt empty after. It didn't satisfy the gnaw or hunger, the sense that something is missing. I may be a fuck up, annihilating my last remaining brain cells with pharmaceutical speed and pot, and relying on my drug dealer to drive me to bookings, but at least I'm not trying to fix the void inside me by being shat on.

I shower and get dressed, wait for Jean Paul. He pulls up outside the hotel, wedges the door open and holds up a bag of lukewarm French fries he's procured for me.

We drive home in silence, listening to Electric Light Orchestra.

'Man, I don't know why you thought this dude was going to keep his eyes closed,' says Jean Paul as I smoke and drink the memory of my client picking my shit out of his lashes. 'That dude wanted the FULL front row viewing.'

We laugh all the rest of the way home.

Girls' trip

Somewhere between the assignments I'm writing and the never-ending winter I fall apart. I can't touch a client; I can't even look at my phone. Brittany and I spend every night together on the couch, wrapped in blankets. Netflix asks us if we are still watching. Sometimes we bundle ourselves in jackets and scarves and walk the three blocks up to the IGA, or the middle eastern restaurant that's open until late. We come home and sit on our sides of the sofa and eat Turkish Delight or blocks of Cadbury Black Forest.

'I'm running out of money,' I say to her one night.

'So am I.'

The winter is eating away at me. I know I need to work, but I can't. I can't become her right now; I feel my bones hollowed out by the cold I can't escape. I feel the weight of the philosophy papers that are due bearing down on me.

I feel the pain of my break-up. My body is physically sick, I have a never-ending cold that won't go away no matter how many garlic cloves I chew.

'I did a double the other day,' says Brittany, picking at her nails on the couch. 'I just didn't feel like me. I rocked up and the other girl, her tan was all fresh and her nails were done, and I could tell she'd just had her lashes filled. I felt so shabby.'

I come up with an idea.

'Why don't we go work somewhere warmer?'

I have a place in mind. My hideaway brothel, the one that the guys from the review boards don't go to and therefore couldn't spot me and post everywhere that I was working back at a brothel. It was tucked away in the Western Suburbs of Sydney. I felt anonymous there. I liked brothel work, I liked going in and out of bookings. I send them a text and photos of us, and we are rostered on for two weeks.

When we arrive in Sydney, we prepare for the two weeks ahead. The key to making the most money on a brothel trip is to keep your overheads to a minimum. I knew how to survive a brothel tour, and it was by going to Coles and getting tins of tuna, bananas, a loaf of bread for toast. Things you could shovel down quickly between clients, just enough to satisfy you and stop you spending $50 on having a carbonara pasta from some dodgy pizza shop. We lug our suitcases from the airport to Central Station, take the train to Parramatta and then a bus to the middle of nowhere.

We've been awake since 6 a.m., and our shift starts at 7 p.m. We will be working until 5 a.m., and be doing this for the next fourteen days. We can choose to take a day off but neither of us would want to, knowing we'd lose our momentum, knowing we'd disrupt that sleeping routine of going to bed at 6 a.m. and waking up at 3 p.m.

The first time I came to this brothel, I was welcomed into the fold very quickly. I'd walk upstairs in my pyjamas, hiding from clients as I scurried to the girls' room. I preferred upstairs because you could smoke up there. I'd bring up my Styrofoam cup with black coffee from the machine, pour my little container of UHT milk into it and talk shit. We'd tan each other's backs and complain about clients and laugh. Somebody would put on the lifestyle channel and we'd sit around, watching *Say Yes to the Dress*. 'Tell me which one she picks!' one of the girls would say, as she sprayed perfume in her hair to disguise the cigarette smoke and ran down to her next booking. At the end of the night we'd all peel off our lashes around the mirrors and take our toiletries bags to the shower block. We'd chat to each other as we showered and dried off, and then we'd all go to the dorms and get into bed. And then do it all over again the next day.

One of the times I went there I became friends with an older woman. We bonded one night over astrology. We would walk together each afternoon to the fruit and vegetable shop about a kilometre away, deep in the suburbs. We'd make dinner together, and we did doubles together.

At the end of the shift we'd stay up and do tarot readings. She told me she came from a line of Indigenous women who knew magic. She told me she sensed I could see things others couldn't. We spoke about love and death and magic and grief and pain and our spirituality in the early morning light, clutching cups of herbal tea. When she left to go home, I cried quietly in the dorm room.

You cry sometimes at brothels. You cry because you're tired, you cry because the receptionist snaps at you, you cry because you've forgotten what the sun looks like after working nights for a week straight. You cry because no matter how many showers you have with sage soap, and regardless of the tiger's eye you carry, the energy starts to get to you. As my older friend said, 'Sadness is in this place. You have to protect yourself from it.'

Cum-filled trash cans, cigarette burns on sheets, men lying and men cheating, signs on the walls telling you all the reasons you might be fired or have your pay withheld. Messages from your ex-boyfriend before your shift starts and you and your best friend are fighting. The client who wouldn't pay for extras and kept trying to go down on you, your thigh muscles cramping from the effort of pushing him away. You've changed your outfit four times and you still aren't being booked, rejected by men you wouldn't touch with a ten-foot pole. You try to hold down the tears because you know that once they start they won't stop and you won't make any money that night, so you go find a quiet corner and try to breathe through it. You think about your friend and wish she was there. The other girls aren't being unkind by not comforting you; it's just that sadness is infectious and they have bills to pay.

Brittany and I think we're prepared, but as the shift goes on, I realise I've forgotten how to do this. The receptionist is, quite simply, a fucking mole. She hates me on sight and I don't know why. My clients are exhausting. One of them tries to fuck me without a condom on and I have to kick him off me. I already have the desire to cry and it's not even midnight yet, not even a full day of work yet. I have thirteen more to go.

When we are finally allowed to go to bed, we take our money from the receptionist where we are paid out, our cards stamped.

'Where are we going to sleep?' we ask the receptionist.

'All the dorm beds are taken. You can have room seven.'

We go to the cupboard to find a blanket but they are all gone. No duvets left, not even a throw rug. I scan around the girls' room and find a polar fleece that's been placed down to protect the seats from fake tan. The window in the shower block won't close and Brittany and I shiver as we quickly dry ourselves off.

The mattress feels like it's made out of granite. I know the other rooms have better, softer beds but I'm too exhausted to go and argue with the tight-lipped sourpuss out the front. I huddle close to Brittany and we curl together for warmth because the heating's turned off now. The fake-tan rug is for a single bed but we both manage to squeeze under it. It's 7 a.m.

I awake to a screaming and bashing. The room is filled with loud drumming and the sound of cymbals crashing together. It's so chaotic that for a second I don't understand where I am. Have I died and gone to hell?

Brittany gets out of bed and stumbles to the wall, bashing the control pad. The screeching stops. The brothel has reopened and the PA system that usually plays Top 40 hits has been turned on, inexplicably, to some kind of drone noise art soundtrack.

It's 10 a.m. We've slept for three hours.

I hear a knock on the door and get up to open it.

'We need this room for bookings,' the receptionist says, 'you girls can move to the dorm now, the day girls are up.'

I close the door in her face and stare at Brittany.

'Fuck this,' she says.

We get all our clothes, our suitcases, our bags of groceries and make-up and we quietly slip out of the dorm room. We take a quick look around the girls' room and check for our hair straighteners, our bottles of lube. We manage to clear out our lockers without anyone noticing and leave the keys in the doors.

Brittany approaches the receptionist desk.

'We've booked a motel room in Parramatta,' she says, her giant sunglasses obscuring her face. 'We are going to go there and get some sleep. We'll be back later for our shift.'

I stand behind Brittany, peering at the psycho reception- ist, holding my breath. I'm petrified she won't let us go, that somebody will come and drag us kicking and screaming into the dorm rooms.

'Of course,' she says, not even looking up from her computer screen. 'See you later.'

Brittany and I slowly wheel our suitcases towards the door, smiling, but as soon as we are in the carpark, we bolt for the waiting Uber.

'Smoke bombed the fuck out of there,' she says.

The Uber pulls on to the freeway and I watch as the gum trees roll away from us, the industrial buildings turn into terrace houses and in the distance, I can see the Westfield Tower and Sydney Harbour Bridge. Relief floods over me and I start laughing and so does Brittany. We are wiping away tears of laughter.

We post doubles specials online while we hunt for a hotel room on Agoda, search for coupon codes. We pool our collective cash from the night before and walk into a corner room, with crisp white linen and a big bathroom with no open windows and soft towels. We buy a bottle of champagne and crack it open while we take turns screening booking enquiries. We fuck strangers together, and when one of us gets a solo booking, the other sits in the lobby and fields the next job. One of our clients comes inside his pants the second we start kissing—it's very cute. Our money pile grows and the screaming music and concrete beds feel like a distant memory (even though it was only eight hours ago). We go downstairs at the end of the day and pay for another night in the hotel.

That night a client takes us out to a strip club. He gets a VIP room and we sit there, drinking, getting lap dances. He pulls out a baggie and we snort lines, our freshly blow-dried hair flicked out of the way as we reach down for the note and the mirror. Later that night I'm back at our client's apartment and one of the strippers has come back with us. She's skateboarding around naked and I'm smoking naked on the balcony, watching people walk around. I look down at my phone and realise it's almost 7 a.m. Brittany and I have a booking at 10 a.m.

'Brittany,' I say, coming inside. 'We have work soon.'

'I'll be fine,' she says. 'I'll meet you at the hotel.'

I send Brittany a photo of myself, smoking out the front of the hotel in a dressing gown and Ray-Bans.

'I'm still cooked,' I type. She sends me back the emoji of the egg frying in the pan. Our brains are scrambled.

I'm having a strong coffee and staring at the patterns in the carpet. The door flies open and it's Brittany, her hair standing on end. We have 30 minutes before our client gets there.

'Find me whatever you can to drink and order me a coffee,' she says before disappearing into the shower. I bring her a mini Bacardi, mini vodka and a double espresso and we do a two-hour booking with a man who doesn't come until the last five minutes.

We have had three hours sleep over the last 48 hours. We've made our rent, our flights home, and a profit. We get into our king-sized bed, draw the shades and take Xanax. It kicks in, I'm warm and sleepy and I snuggle up close to Brittany as we watch *The OC* on my laptop.

'Dude,' I say, 'how fucking fun was that?'

Whore beauty

Shave your junk

Men's razors. The Gillette sensitive kind. If you use women's razors you end up with stubble and razor burn. Sit on the floor of your shower, cover your pussy in shaving foam, and always shave in the direction of the hair growth. Pull the skin taut and don't forget about the bikini line. You won't slice your clit off if you shave over your labia but don't apply the same pressure as you would to the rest. Don't skimp on the shaving foam but if you're all out, hair conditioner works too. Shave from in to out around your butthole. The trick to not getting enormous ingrown hairs is to rub after wax moisturiser into your pussy when you get out of the shower. You want the kind that beauty therapists use but anything with tea tree oil in it will work.

Fuck on your period

How much time do you have? If the booking's that night, go to the sex shop. Don't go to the busiest one, especially around a full moon, because you'll climb the stairs, go to the counter and—in a hushed voice—ask for menstrual sponges and they'll say, *we just sold our last one*. Every hooker in town has her period and they've all come to the same Club X on Bourke Street to get a sponge before disappearing into Crown Towers or The Hyatt. You have to go to the Crazyhorse Cinema, the peepshow on Elizabeth Street. When you walk down the stairs, you can hear the sound of women moaning and screaming from behind velvet curtains. There's a rhythmic thudding and lube suctioning and popping. There's a booth where you pay for tokens but the guy there always has sponges in stock, because it smells like semen and air freshener, and nobody wants to go in there. Scurry out with your big bag of sponges (never buy one, always get them in bulk). Or stroll out, because you don't care. You like that it's sleazy.

Get in the shower, squat, and use one of the long acrylic nails on your fingers to scoop out the clots of blood from your vagina. Watch in fascination at the black matter that slides down your fingers and turns to pink foam in the drain. Once you've scraped your pussy clean, insert the sponge like a tampon. Push it as far up as it can go without it getting lost.

Last-minute booking? Car sponge, chopped into a square. Even less time? Kitchen sponge, the one with the thick foam and the scourer on the other side. Chop the scourer off and cut a square of foam. Boil it if you have the time.

I should have told you earlier, when you were at the cinema, to get the pink condoms. Blood turns into girl cum. Pink condoms make it invisible. I always forget and I'm a heavy bleeder, so as soon as I hop off a hard condom-covered dick (never in reverse cowgirl or doggy—too easy for them to spot the bloody condoms) I bring my hand down to jerk them off, whipping the condom off in one fell swoop and then I toss it to the other end of the room. Pink condom now.

The clients least likely to be freaked out by your period are the ones who're married with children. Those are my favourites.

Get rid of BV

You bare-backed your boyfriend, didn't you? I don't blame you; it feels good. I've spent eight years fucking with condoms on and now I've developed a cream pie fetish. I'm a sick freak, perverted by safe sex. When I get into a monogamous relationship all I want is my lover to fuck me and fill me with cum. I want to go to the toilet and pee out cum. Porn stars get to, why can't hookers? But you pay a price for that cream pie when the acidity of your lover's cum throws off your pH balance. Expect a double down on that when you are home in your sweatpants, free bleeding and watching a movie and he walks in, in his hi-vis shirt, smelling like sweat and with calloused hands from working all day. He pulls your comfortable pants off you and fucks you on the couch, fucks you bloody all over the throw rug. Pink cum.

The next day you're preparing to work, you are peeing and then the smell hits you. Somewhere between a piece of salmon left out in the sun and vinegar, a wet pussy but not the kind you like. See, if you were smart, you'd already have a packet of Flagyl in the cupboard. My favourite is the pack of five which you take in one fell swoop and kills every speck of bacteria but will also make you projectile vomit if you have a glass of wine before your booking. You don't have the Flagyl, because you always forget to ask for a repeat. Make an appointment at the bulk-billing clinic in the taxi on the way to the hotel.

No time? Buy a bottle of Pump water and some apple cider vinegar. Take off the lid, tip out a bit of the water and add a capful of the vinegar to the water. Put the lid back on, and douche with that. It's semi sterile (I think).

(I take no responsibility for any of this medical advice.)

Deal with thrush

You've taken the Flagyl and your pH is back to regular. The antibiotics have killed all the good bacteria in your body and now candida has taken over. You fantasise about scratching the inside of your vagina with a steel baby bottle cleaner. Your favourite undies are ruined. The thrush is so bad that when you wipe, your pussy feels like sandpaper. You also need to work tomorrow.

Try not to make a salad in your pussy. Shoving garlic or coconut oil or yoghurt might soothe it for a minute but then it stops working. The candida eats the sugars in the coconut oil and multiplies. The yoghurt (natural, no sugar) works better if you just eat it. The garlic . . . well, I never quite understood that one. It just left my vagina smelling like a warm souvlaki.

Go to the chemist. Get the oral tablet, generic brand. Get the Canesten cream or tablets you insert up in your pussy. When they say, have you had this before? Just lie. 'Only once or twice,' you say, quietly, so you don't have to tell the entire queue your slutty medical history. One time, my burning vagina and brain a hungover, pounding mess, I hissed at them, 'What, you got a cure for chronic thrush back there I don't know about?'

Sit at home, in your big cotton undies, with a sanitary pad on and your pussy smeared in the cream that stops you from scratching it raw. The sanitary pad is there because in the morning, when you wake up, the pellet of Canesten will have dissolved and your vagina is expelling it. Not fun to clean off your sheets, trust me.

Ass pimples

Have you ever dragged a fingertip along a strip club's stage and then inspected what's on it? No, because you aren't insane. Let me tell you—grime. Dirt. Bacteria. Dried sweat.

Baby powder from girls clapping their hands together before climbing the pole. Tiny wood splinters from the lacquered floor and spilt sugary drinks that get tracked on the soles of 8-inch clear heels. You are rolling in that. Then when you are done rolling, you go and grind your bare ass on men's laps and their dirty jeans. You do that for eight hours, ten hours, twelve hours. The next morning you wake up and see it. A big, red zit right on the middle of your ass cheek. You turn and look at your chest—peppered with tiny scratches from stubble grazing it. Another cluster of pimples starting to pop up.

Come home and wash your whole body with Cetaphil and then apply a thick layer of Benzac.

Haemorrhoids

You did an anal booking today, and it hurt. You don't know what happened; maybe you weren't in the mood. You go to the toilet when the client leaves and you fart out silicon lube and go to wipe, and then you feel it. Your butthole feels chewed up and spat out. You remember the line from that Sheila Jeffreys book you had to read (to counter argue) at university, where she talked about going to the strip club and staring at 'swollen anuses' and you were like, *Sheila, what the fuck are you talking about?*

The haemorrhoid gets bigger and bigger. It feels like a tiny grape hanging out of your butthole. *What the fuck,* you think, staring at it in the mirror. Because you've never had one before you freak out and make a doctor's appointment. You can't sit properly on the hard, plastic chair in the waiting room. You know that if you tell the doctor it was from doing anal at work, she'll be weird. Backing away from you and putting gloves on just to speak to you, applying hand sanitiser as soon as she has to touch your arm to take your blood pressure.

So you say 'Oh my boyfriend and I did anal,' as you bend over to show her your haemorrhoid. She starts telling you that you need a colonoscopy to check there aren't more up there. You decide not to tell her you are well acquainted with the passage of your rectum, considering you stick a finger up there every time you douche to check you didn't miss anything.

You leave with a script, and a referral for a colonoscopy. You look down at the referral sheet you have to hand the front desk and in big, capital letters it says 'ANAL SEX CAUSED HAEMORRHOIDS.' You decide not to hand it over. You'll take the chance on this one.

Massage oil

The massage parlour hands you a huge, squidgy bottle. The oil is a sinister, murky pale yellow and slick to the touch. You are supposed to do your body slides and wank men off with this mysterious liquid. You get into the room and do your thing, slippery and wet. It gets in your freshly washed and blow-dried hair. It gets in your pussy, on your asshole, on your face. When you finish at the end of the day, you stand in the shower and have to lather and rinse twice and you still feel sticky. As you leave you notice all the other girls have bulk-sized bottles of Sorbolene moisturiser. The next day you wake up and your entire back and boobs are covered in cystic acne. You go back to work, covered in concealer and foundation and pick up your bottle from the counter. You take off the lid and sniff it. You know this smell and you can't place it. A girl catches you doing your own personal sommelier experience and leans over to you.

'It's vegetable oil,' she says.

You go to Coles and buy a bulk-sized bottle of Sorbolene. Your acne goes away.

Keep your face on

You have three bookings, one after the other at the brothel. You get there early, so you can sit and do your make-up. It's perfect, your first face. You primed, you buffed your foundation in, did a perfect contour and baked under your eyes. Your eyeliner is winged and your lashes, applied with tweezers, are flicked out perfectly. Highlighter on the cupid's bow, the cheekbone, and in the corner of your eyes to disguise that you didn't sleep last night. You don't put on lipstick because you aren't a fucking amateur. Clear gloss. You don't apply a setting spray. You need this make-up runny.

You come down from your booking and you have two minutes before your next one.

The first time, all you need to do is mash your foundation brush around your mouth where the client licked off all your make-up. You use the back of your hand to wipe the foundation from your lips and drag the brush under your eye to pick up the mascara flecks.

The second time you mash foundation around your mouth and over your whole face. You go at warp speed, dragging bronzer into the paste on your skin, a heavy contour but nobody will notice in this light. While you're doing all this, Listerine burns in your mouth. Spit in the sink and readjust the lash that's starting to flick out.

Your third client is your favourite. He face-fucks you until your mascara runs, he flips you over like a rag doll and fucks you holding your face into the pillow. Have you ever wondered why brothels have such dark linen? It's because of sluts like me who like being brutally fucked by some towering tradie and slobbering on to the pillow as my eyes roll in the back of my head. If that was white . . . you come, even if you didn't mean to. You go back downstairs with your hair sticking out, an eyelash stuck to your cheek and your work wife gives you a look in the mirror as she's doing her lip liner.

'Good booking?' she says.

'Mmm,' you say.

You don't even care about your face at this point. You mash, peel off the lashes and buff the remainder of the winged liner in.

You go back out and get booked again and again. Not because your make-up is perfect but because you smell like a woman who just came. David Attenborough narrates over the top, *the other males in the pack sense the female is on heat and seek to mate with her.*

Prep for anal
One time I was on this Facebook feminist group and somebody asked how everyone prepared for anal sex. I felt my fingers fly across the keyboard, my favourite how-to ever. A girl commented on my post and she told me everything I said was wrong, dangerous and incorrect. *I'm a nurse*, she says. *Well bitch*, I reply, *I'm a whore and this is how I make my money.*

You aren't going to shit on them. The only time you will shit on them is if you do the cocaine they got from South America, brought back in a tiny vial in their suit jacket. You'll shit on them because even though you did everything to prepare for that booking, that was really good cocaine. The coke was so good the client who gave it to you wouldn't stop following you around his beautiful, architecturally designed home complete with beautiful marble bathrooms with beautiful toilets without any beautiful doors. A shiny object distracts him, and you bolt downstairs, ready to expel your bowels that felt empty up until you hit that second fat line. You only get to take half a shit because he's back again, clutching a bottle of red wine and you have to stop, wipe and quickly flush before he notices.

You'll shit all over him because you are high as a kite, watching porn on his projector, him fucking you in the ass and you come and then look over at the beautiful white linen. *Oh dear*, you think. He doesn't book you again.

In short:

Insert one Microlax up your ass. Spit on your fingers beforehand and lube up your asshole. Don't take oral laxatives because you'll shit for hours.

Start having your shower. Wait anywhere between 1–15 minutes before you feel your stomach grip and fling yourself onto the toilet bowl. Shit.

Get back in the shower, and start lathering yourself in body wash before realising you need to shit again.

Do this until you shit out the sign there's nothing left up there. It's a viscous, mucus ass booger—like a big snot. It's better to get that out now, because otherwise it might attach itself to a butt plug and when you pull that plug out, it will fly across the room like an Olympic gymnast and land neatly on the bed.

Take a douche with warm water, not hot. Hot water will set fire to your sphincter. Get into doggy position, head closer to the ground. Squirt till you can't squirt anymore, get up, and fart into toilet bowl. Inspect. Do this until the water is clear.

If you want to take one last extra precaution—spit on finger and put up butthole. Remove, check.

Maybe this is why I get haemorrhoids. Maybe that nurse was right.

Look good under stage lights

Ignore everything the beauty blogger who wants dewy skin for her stroll down the French Riviera says. Skip straight to the tutorial for drag queens. Drag queens can teach you a lot about doing your face for the strip club. Queens are painting for stage lighting and dark clubs. They are painting for the back row, and sometimes it's the guy sitting the furthest from the stage with the most money to spend.

Cop a load to the face

You are kneeling on the floor of the hotel room. If you're lucky, the carpet is soft. If it's not, which is how it usually goes, you're already starting to get burns. You don't have to break the mood—just grab a towel from the bed and place it under your knees so the cleaner doesn't have to scrub semen from the floor the next day.

'Oh yeah,' he says, jacking off and looking down at you.

Don't say; *don't get it in my eyes*. It's pointless. Men cannot aim when they come, unlike the professional porn star he's watched countless times. He thinks he can, but he's going to get cum in your hair, up your nose and most definitely, in the middle of your retina.

Find the sweet spot between staring up at him with your big, come-fuck-me eyes and also at his ball sack and dick. If you stare at them too much, they get stage fright. If you don't look at them, they'll lose their hard-on or think you are disinterested.

'I want you to blow a big load all over my face,' you say, as you lick their balls. You just want to go home, to be honest. There's a new episode of *Married at First Sight* you want to watch. This one has been hard work—you've fucked like it's an Olympic sport. You know this is a guy who watches so much porn he's forgotten what it's like to use something other than his hand to come. You could literally be his favourite porn star, right there in the flesh and he'd still have to finish this way.

'Ughhhh,' he says.

'Oh yeah babe,' you say, 'are you gonna come? Come all over my slutty whore mouth. I wanna be your fucking cum rag.'

At this point, tilt your chin back, open your mouth and stick out your tongue and close your eyes that have a full set of freshly done Russian volumes. Pray to god that he aims nose down and not on your lashes.

He's jizzed on your nose, your cheeks; it's on your tongue. Keep your eyes shut and ask for a towel, which he will race to get you. Keep your eyes closed, bring your hands up to your eyes first. Check if there's any cum, and if there is, wipe the towel gently down. Don't rub. Open eyes, make sure they aren't burning, and remove rest in bathroom. Try not to gag on the taste of his jizz. Roll whatever's left away from your taste buds (the middle of my tongue works best for me) and hack it into the sink. Do not let it simmer for your senses to pick up. Whatever you do, don't think about that one porno you saw where twenty guys jacked off into a Vitamix blender and it was just this slurry of greyish semen and then BRRRRR goes the blender and then that girl chugged it, and you ran to the bathroom and threw up while your friend laughed hysterically.

Fix yourself for an overnight when you've left your toiletries at home

Your client has extended and wants you to stay the night at his hotel. You are getting along so well, he wants to spend more time with you, and it feels good. Until you realise you don't have your cleanser, your deodorant, a hairbrush or even a toothbrush.

You are not blessed with the epidermis of a supermodel or even a mere mortal. You have skin that explodes with clusters of pimples from just one night of sleeping in your foundation.

It's time for bed and you look in your whore handbag. Please god, you think, let me have it packed in here. You find it, the comb you swiped from the hotel you were at last time, the hotel with the little drawers of brushes and cotton pads that you dearly wish you were at right now. Use it to detangle the knots in your hair from the hours of sex you've had.

You also have baby wipes—and his toothbrush. You use it, and don't tell him.

Take the bar of astringent hotel hand soap and use a hot flannel (not the one you wiped your pussy with earlier), and double cleanse. Your face feels like sandpaper. Mascara runs down your cheeks. You use the baby wipe, more burning, to clean your eyes. Moisturise with the lavender smelling body lotion and wince as you think about the paraben and alcohol content and hope to god there's a shred of lanolin in there.

Come back to bed, and when your client sees you, looking pink and raw, he says, you look pretty without make-up on. You hope he can't see the acne scarring or the purple bags under your eyes or the zit you picked in the bathroom in the magnifying mirror, strategically placed next to the hand soap.

Come down from a coke booking

It's 7 a.m. You notice some of the girls trying to be a wifey and cleaning up these idiots' empty bottles of Grey Goose and putting away their coke plates. You know it's time to leave when that starts happening. You aren't cleaning up jack shit, but you know why they are doing it. The coke buzz has worn off and all that's left is the gritty ampheta-mine alertness, just hands looking for things to do to stop the buzz in your brain. You are out of here. This isn't your first rodeo. You glance back at the newbie hooker, who's stacking the dishwasher in the penthouse apartment. You are torn between putting her purse in her hand, her coat around her shoulders and stuffing her in a taxi, and swiping the plate out of her hand and telling her to snap out of it. When did you become so hardened?

You have your sunglasses with you, because you knew it was a party booking. You also have a coat, because you want to look less like a coked-out prostitute as you hail a taxi at 8 a.m. on a busy main road while people who look like the guys you just fucked go to work.

Years ago, you would have tied one on. You would have texted one of your friends who's always up for it, bought another bag and sat down on the balcony, wrapped in a dressing gown. You would have made Bloody Marys, with tabasco and fresh wedges of lemon. You and your friend would have played Fleetwood Mac, instead of that rhythmic, heart palpitating techno you've just listened to all night. Your friend would get the same buzz you had fifteen hours ago and you would have just felt more awake. Your teeth start to grit, and you wonder if you should have just gone to bed instead.

You're older and wiser now and you know the serotonin and dopamine stores, what little you have as a depressive, are gone. They've been mined, and you need to go home.

The best way to come down is to clean.

You get into your apartment, and your cat runs between your legs. You pick it up and press its fur to your face and hear it purring loudly. You stand like that for a while, rocking your cat back and forth.

Draw the blinds. Put on Fleetwood Mac, but quietly. Take out the trash, stack your own dishwasher, and put away your make-up that's strewn by your mirror. Strip the bed and remake it with fresh linen, spray lavender oil all over your pillows. Light candles, burn incense, sage your room. Feed the cat, empty its litter box. Use every last scrap of your nervous, anxious coked out energy to make your house cosy and inviting again.

Get into the shower and have it hot. Scrub yourself from head to toe, wash your make-up off, tone and moisturise. Put on your soft pyjama pants, your big band t-shirt. Brew a pot of camomile tea and open your 'medicine' box. You've got a stash in there. Xanax, you think, that's what I feel like.

Sit down on your couch, your cat on your lap, your house perfect and clean, your cup of tea and your Xanax kicking in. You're going to feel a bit shit, a bit edgy, a bit fucked still, but cartoons are helping and so is the fact that on your coffee table sits a big wad of cash.

Put a condom on
You are in a booking with another girl at the brothel. Clients do that sometimes, point at you and some other random girl and say, 'you two.' You and the girl look at each other. You've said hi once or twice, but now you have to fuck each other and him.

After some fooling around it's time to fuck and you go to get the condom, clumsy and all thumbs. She sees you, takes it and rips the corner with her teeth, spitting the foil out the side of her mouth like some old-time cowboy gunslinger shooting tobacco into a spittoon. She pops the condom in her mouth and rolls it onto the guy's cock using her lips.

Holy fuck, you think, *that's impressive.*

Wash your expensive lingerie

You pull the set of lingerie you spent three bookings worth of money on out of the washing machine. It was white lace and now it's the colour of old gym socks. The lace has pilled and greyed from the black sock you didn't notice.

FUCK, you scream, into the empty apartment. Your cat stares at you.

Go to the supermarket and get a plastic bucket. If you don't have one, you can use the tin container that comes with your rice cooker, which you do for several years because you never make rice anyway. You get a capful of wool wash and a nail scrubbing brush and you separate the reds, whites and blacks and hand wash them in your rice cooker bowl. Use the nail scrubber on the crotches of your expensive lingerie to get rid of girl cum and fake tan and period stains from when your sponge leaked. On the tough ones, apply a paste of Napisan for colours and let it sit. Don't put them on your communal clothesline because your pervert neighbour will steal them to jack off into. Drape them over the couch in your apartment and let the central heating do its job.

When a client rapes you

Sit at the bottom of your shower and let the water pound down on your back. Try to imagine the night washing off you and going down the drain like your friend said. You can still feel it, the weight of that body bearing down on you, holding you in place. The memory shifts, you second-guess yourself. Was I raped, you think, or am I imagining things? A memory of something you read, about the further you are away from the woman dragged down the alley by a stranger, the less credible you become.

Sit at the bottom of the shower and try to cry but you can't. You have learnt now that you have to keep going on because if you let this break you every time you'd never work again.

Sit at the bottom of the shower and think about your ex-boyfriend and wish he was here right now to fold you into your bed and remind you that not all men are evil.

Sit at the bottom of the shower and wrap your arms around your naked thighs and curl into a tight little ball and try to come back into your body.

Sit at the bottom of the shower until you can stand again.

LOVE

Good sex

I've worked the last two nights in a row. On Thursday I did a double booking. On Friday I went to Crown Casino and I did a two-hour booking, showered, reapplied my make-up in his bathroom and then went to do a two-hour party booking. The party booking had two other girls there and everyone was doing coke. I made an excuse as to why I couldn't—fake heart condition, babysitting, whatever came to mind. I wasn't in the mood to be high and jittery.

This morning I take myself out for smashed avocado and eggs, with a strong espresso. I sit and stare out of the window. My body aches. I feel sadness wash over me as I poke into the egg yolks and watch them spread across my plate. It's a hangover breakfast, something needed to soak up the champagne from last night. The sadness is both chemically induced and stemming from my mind replaying the angry messages I sent last night—drunk, naked and hunched over my phone at the end of my booking. In the background, the other girls were talking in that hurried, coked-out way and this guy I'm seeing asked if I wanted to come over and watch a movie.

Sure, I replied, *but I'm just at work now. I'll be done at 12.*

I watch the screen and I can see him typing. He starts again and then stops. I begin to chew my nail right at the corner where it hurts.

I don't know. I'm getting tired now. I'm not sure how I feel about being fitted in after work. Let's do another night.

My phone dings, drawing me from my trance, and it's a booking request. Can I come to South Yarra? Will I eat ass if he pays me extra?

I can feel my period sitting in the crotch of my G-string. I don't have time to go to the sex shop and buy a menstrual sponge. I head home, go to the trash can in the bathroom and dig out a bloody piece of sea sponge I used the night before, and put it in a saucepan. I bring it to the boil and watch as a grey foam rises to the surface. When I pull out the sponge, it's shrunken into a tiny little pebble. I picture myself in the ER, a doctor having to pull it out with forceps as my cervix tries to swallow it. The convenience store on the corner sells thick kitchen sponges and I decide to try that instead. I slice the scourer end off with my chef's knife and cut the sponge into a circle. I shower and moisturise, apply my deodorant and then squat down on the floor, pushing the kitchen sponge up my pussy.

It's a quick booking, just an hour, I tell myself. It'll be a straight up and down kind of fuck. I fear that if I start saying no, the well will dry up. That there's some kind of law in physics that means when I'm too tired, I'll cause a gravitational shift in my currency flow. Just make some small talk, Rita, and then say, let's head to the bedroom.

When he opens the door to let me in, I look him up and down. Sometimes I can see a look in somebody's eyes that draws me in when they open the door. Desire, an appraisal, relief. There wasn't anything in his eyes.

We make small talk, and he draws out his words long and slow. He's a country boy and he's not much older than me. We use the spare room in his apartment and it's bare. No cover on the doona, mismatched linen-covered pillows. He hands me the money and I set up my things. I lay out my speaker, my iPhone, my bag of condoms and I plug the Hitachi vibrator into the wall. 'I like your lingerie,' he says. 'My wife was really into lingerie, I used to buy it for her all the time.'

'You were married?'

'Yeah. Not anymore though.'

He is undressing behind me, we talk over our shoulders as we both strip off, our backs facing each other. I climb onto the bed and it's an old, soft mattress. I find this and the slightly musty scent of the doona strangely calming. It feels lived in.

He lies in the centre of the bed and I do what I always do, climb on top and lean in to kiss him. I'm surprised when he runs his hands softly down my back, following the vertebrae of my spine. He kisses me deeply and softly, brings his hands up to cradle my face in them.

'You are so gorgeous,' he says to me. I look up at him and I can see that he means it.

His hands move around my shoulders, down my thighs, finding small crooks in the curves of my body to rest into. His touch is intimate and familiar. I find myself making involuntary noises of pleasure, find myself meeting his kisses with unexpected desire. My tiredness begins to wash away and I find a renewed sense of urgency. His hands become more forceful as he pushes my neck away from him, he kisses it hard and holds me down. It's at this point that I realise he will be fucking me today, and not the other way around.

So, I allow myself to be fucked. I give myself over to the experience of having somebody else choreograph the routine I usually piece together. Wherever he touches me, I allow myself to be present there. It is here that I'm struck by how easy it is for me to lose myself at work, when I'm Gia. How it used to be the other way around, before Peter and James died. Now I know the risk of allowing anyone to get too close to me in my personal life. I'm acutely aware of what's at stake. I know this person likes me because he could have bent me over the bed, fucked me hard and fast and pushed me out the door. I know he finds me attractive because he's telling me so, while I'm blowing him, while he's fucking me. You are so gorgeous, he says over and over again, and like a sponge I soak it all up. I don't believe these things about myself but when somebody is paying me I can. I don't question it. He doesn't need to lie to me, I suppose.

There's something sad too, about a stranger caring more about my body, caring more about pleasuring me, than somebody I voluntarily give my time too. He shows me tenderness and the person I like is treating me like a whore. I think about that text message again and wonder what he meant. Am I a different person when I go to work if I come home to somebody after?

The client has my legs between his and he's fucking me well, exactly how I like to be fucked. Rough and loving all at once, and I can feel myself getting closer to coming. Suddenly, he pulls out of me and flips me over, wrenches the condom off and comes all over my chest.

'That was a bit of fun, wasn't it?' He gets up and goes to get some toilet paper for me.

I lie on the bed and stare at the ceiling.

He comes back in and hands me the toilet paper and I clean myself up. He stands there awkwardly.

'How much time do we have left?'

I check my iPhone.

'Ten minutes?'

'I'm pretty tired now after that.'

I want to keep being fucked. I want him to make me come. I want him to fuck me the way I wish people would fuck me, with kindness and interest and desire. I want to stay in that place where my mind is gloriously blank and all I can think about is how good whatever is happening to my body feels. I can hear *South Park* playing on the TV in the lounge room and I wish he would ask me to stay and watch it with him. Order a pizza. I would put my head in his lap, and he would play with my hair. I would sit there in my $175 satin and silk G-string and he'd find me an old sweater of his to wear to keep me warm.

'Would . . . would you want to fuck again?'

He pauses to think.

'No, I'm pretty tired. Normally I'm a real in-and-out kind of guy.'

'You are a really great fuck.'

'Aw. I don't think so.'

'No, you are. You're great. That was the best sex I've had in ages.'

'I dunno. I think when you are married for so long, that's the kind of sex you get used to having. Loving, I suppose.'

I begin to wonder if I am overstaying my welcome. I think about asking him about his marriage but I don't want to ruin the moment. I want to think he fucked me like that because he cared about me.

So I pack up my iPhone, my condoms and my Hitachi. I dress myself facing away from him, as he does to me.

He walks me to the elevator, and we kiss each other on the cheek goodbye.

When I get downstairs, it's raining outside, so I sit in the foyer as I wait for my taxi. I sit on the stairs and I wonder when I'll feel that way again, with somebody who isn't paying me to be there.

Eighteen

A friend of mine once said that the abuse and the love story are two separate entities. They weave into one another, they get tangled together, but they are ultimately different stories.

Here is the love story.

Peter wasn't answering his phone. I was at Flinders Street Station, thinking about my house key, sitting on the kitchen table where I'd left it that morning.

I had company though, on my Facebook Messenger. I'd been chatting to Todd for a few weeks now. So far all I knew of him were his tattooed shins.

'Why don't you come here?' he replied.

When I arrived at his house, he opened the door and I finally got to see his face. Blue eyes and these slightly crooked but very white teeth.

We walk to the bottle shop together, trying to make conversation. He gets beers, I get a case of UDLs. We down them quickly, one after another. He suggests we go painting.

I had a definite type. I liked guys with shaved heads and funny teeth. I liked that they were rough and I liked that they were loud, and I liked the casual misogyny of never being allowed to do graffiti with them, only watch and keep a look out for cops or people walking their dogs. I liked their big dicks and their big mouths, and I liked to think that the hardness they exhibited was an act, instead of an overarching view of the world and the women in it.

Todd takes me by the hand, he's feeling more confident now, and we walk down the road, through the scrub and into an abandoned mansion. He boosts me up to push me in through the window and we arrive in what would have been the master bedroom. Todd's rummaging through his green bag, the cans of paint clinking, and I'm getting drunker. The room only has the small window and the smell of paint fills the room. I lie down, clutching my UDL can, and pass out.

Todd shakes me awake and scoops me off the floor. I've been out for a while. I look up, and he's painted my name all over the walls. *Rita, Rita, Rita,* with love hearts and stars, in pinks and whites and baby blues.

I want him to squeeze every bad booking out of me with his arms. Muscle memories of clients kissing and touching my skin, as I grip him tighter. Imprint new ones on me, I think.

'What's up?' he says, his jaw on top of my head.

'I don't think I like escorting.' I am surprised the words come out of my mouth.

'Then,' he says, kissing the top of my head, 'you should stop.'

———

I have found a room on King Street in the city. What once was an office space above a 7-Eleven is now a domestic living quarter, thanks to the introduction of a flimsy shower in the tiny bathroom. The shower's hot water runs out after four minutes, so washing my hair or shaving my legs becomes a choice I have to make every day. Todd moves into my room on a Saturday, and we spend the day organising and setting up his things. As we curl up into bed with our take-away Indian and I hit play on *The OC*, we hear a faint doofing noise that grows louder and louder. I open the window and poke my head out, and the sound of RnB music fills the room. If my bed wasn't in the room, I would assume I was eating take-away in the middle of a club. I quickly realise my bedroom backs onto the court-yard of Men's Gallery, a popular strip club, and that sound travels quite easily through the plaster walls. Todd and I spend a sleepless night listening to 'YEAAAAAAH BOY' screeched from the smokers' area. The next Saturday, and the ones following that, we go joyriding, digging through the hard rubbish to find hidden gems in the rich suburban trash, coming home only when the last straggler is booted from the club.

Todd would text me every morning to say that he loved me, and he hoped I had a good day. He never sent the same text. He'd say that he loved my laugh, or that I made him a better person, or that being with me made him happier than he'd ever been before.

When I stopped sex work and got a job at a clothes store, our combined income dropped. Todd sat up and made a spreadsheet on Excel and factored in everything from the cost of our groceries to money for date nights to me being able to buy new clothes. He budgeted so we never went without.

In the summer when we first met, he would meet me after work to go to the supermarket. Todd loved to cook, and he also loved to steal. He'd pick out the most expensive blue cheese, the best cuts of meat at the deli, the juiciest black olives, fresh herbs and the artisan sourdough. Then he'd stroll over to the self-service check out and put every single item through as potatoes. He'd pack it into a picnic basket, and we'd sit under a tree in Flagstaff Gardens and eat our dinner on the grass. He'd get me to sit in between his legs and put his arms around my waist, and we'd pick at the last of the cheese as we people watched.

Todd made me laugh. He made me laugh so hard I'd cry, doubled over and clutching my stomach.

We had no money, even with our spreadsheet. Every dollar we made went out again, but we would scrimp and save and make sure we could go on a date night every week. Todd went without takeaway coffees so I could have one each morning.

Todd loved going op shopping, and we'd spend hours in the most affluent suburbs on the train lines, digging through the racks to find things to wear. We'd sort through designer clothing with the tags still on it, helping each other pick the perfect piece.

Sometimes we'd borrow Peter's car and go driving at night. We'd listen to tape cassettes. I learnt all the words to 'Kick in the Door' as we'd drive up and down Beach Road, stopping to take bread or milk deliveries from the front of cafes.

Every night, we would get into bed together and put on *Gossip Girl*, or *The OC*, or *Sex and the City*. I would curl up next to Todd and fall asleep with my face to his back. The sound of his breathing worked on me like a tranquilliser.

It was these everyday acts of normality and comfort that made me believe that we were OK.

Todd didn't like sex work. I had this beautiful teal bra and matching lace G-string from Elle Macpherson Intimates. With my long red hair, I felt like Ariel the mermaid when I wore it. I put it on after I had a shower, pulling my dress over it. When I came into the bedroom, Todd placed his arms around my waist, skimming his hands up my thighs and lifting the fabric. He pulled it off over my head and then dropped his hands.

'Why do you have that fucking whore underwear on? Are you planning on fucking somebody else tonight?'

Todd was my first real boyfriend, the first time I'd ever lived with somebody, the first time I felt I was truly loved by someone. I kept doing topless waitressing and bucks parties, but when I got home, he'd be waiting up for me. I would go to hug him, and his body would stiffen. He'd wait for me to shower and I'd stand there, washing the glitter and fake tan off me. My lashes placed back in their tray. I'd look at myself in the mirror, skin pink from scrubbing so hard. Watching the pink foam go down the drain from where my mouth spat it from scrubbing the night off. Putting on the pink little girl pyjamas he liked on me. That's when he would touch me again, when I was clean.

When we weren't fighting about sex work, we were fucking each other. Todd was obsessed with making me come. I was eighteen and I'd only had two orgasms in my sexual relationships with men. The very first was with a guy on a fold-out couch (years later, I would understand the complex geometry of my G-spot and his curved banana dick). The second time I squirted and thought I'd pissed in the guy's mouth. My orgasms were involuntary and rare. Todd wanted one every time we fucked, and if I didn't come, the sex was a waste of time. He would throw me off him and storm off to finish himself in the bathroom. I learnt that if I shut my eyes tight and focused, I could go through my pervert Rolodex. The image that played over and over in my mind the first time

I had an orgasm with Todd was that of my stripper friend's enormous tits bouncing up and down. I thought about her boobs smothering my face, her leaning down to kiss me, slipping her hands into my underwear. Once I worked out I could come by leaving my body, the room, the planet and go to a place full of canings by Colin Firth, being slapped by titties or a bukkake scene of perverts in the VHS section of a sex shop, the orgasms were plentiful. They were never with Todd though, and in the years following, they were never really with the people inside me.

I had a porn shoot scheduled. It was with a friend, Jessie. When I arrived at her house and she ran into my arms to envelope me in a bear hug, I felt relieved. I had been carrying a weight with me, the weight of being branded as a freak by society and by my boyfriend, and it felt good to be around my people. Her boyfriend was the videographer behind her popular website, and he had set up a huge inflatable pool in the lounge room filled with baby oil for us to wrestle and fuck in. We took selfies and cracked up as we slid butt naked around the pool, tripping over each other. I felt a happiness I hadn't experienced in a long time, and as I looked at my friend, I also felt envious. What would it be like, I thought, to come home and not have to rub your skin raw? To have somebody who didn't just tolerate, but embraced your whoredom? I didn't want to leave their house, where I was wrapped up in this cocoon of understanding and acceptance. I had forgotten to check my phone all day, and as we sat down after shooting to eat, I fished it out of my purse. I had dozens of missed calls from Todd.

'I did something stupid,' he says on the voicemail, 'but it's your fault. You did that shoot today.'

Jessie and her boyfriend look at the ceiling, the floor, anywhere but at me. Todd's voice fills the room.

'It's your fault,' he says again, and then he hangs up.

———

I was standing in the bathroom mirror, staring at my chest. My breasts felt rounder and heavier, and when I looked down at my belly, I could see a faint brown line sliced straight down the centre. I turned to the side and placed my hands under my belly button.

Todd walks in.

'You look pregnant,' he says.

We walk to the store and buy two pregnancy tests. I sit and chug a whole bottle of water, and then Todd watches as I piss on the little stick. We rest it on the counter and sit in silence as we wait for the three minutes to be up.

Todd lunges for the stick and turns it to show me. Two lines.

I look up at him, and he passes it to me. I hold the pee-soaked stick and watch as it dribbles onto the tiles. I'm pregnant.

He brings me into his arms and holds me tight. We stand there locked together.

'I'm so happy,' he says.

The hardest part was the morning sickness. If somebody left dirty dishes in the sink, I could smell them from the other side of the King Street flat. I'd have to rush from the bedroom to the bathroom to throw up, retching from the scent of passata sauce or cooked onion. The smell of fresh coffee, one of my favourite things in the world, made me nauseous. I was constantly exhausted, faint and also the horniest I'd ever been in my life. I could not fuck Todd enough.

I threw my cigarettes in the trash can as soon as I saw the positive test. I drank decaf and took vitamins every morning. I borrowed parenting books from the library. I wanted to do everything I could to become the best mother I could be, yet, the challenge of being an eighteen-year-old parent barely crossed my mind. I assumed being a mother would not be dissimilar to owning a pet or perhaps even a plant. I would silence any creeping doubt with learning about sleep school or cognitive functioning in children, but as time went on, a small part of me was asking, are you sure? I pushed that thought deep down inside.

Overnight, my breasts became a full 10G cup. I felt like binding my chest to stop my nipples grazing against anything and sending a shoot of pain down my body. I took a little bit of the money we had and went to the DFO near our apartment. The shop assistant fitted me for a new bra, and it felt good to tell a stranger I was pregnant. She said she was happy for me. I left the store and texted Todd, who was heading out to get some food.

He was with his friend Jasmine, a girl I hadn't met before. As I crossed the road to meet them, I looked at Jasmine and remembered what I felt like before I met Todd. She had her make-up perfectly applied. My own skin was bare, how Todd told me he liked it. She was clutching shopping bags and the two of them were talking and laughing.

'Jasmine has a date,' Todd explained, 'so I helped her pick an outfit.' Jasmine did a twirl, showing off what they'd picked out. Her long legs were clad in sheer denier black tights, a pair of denim cut-offs worn over the top, and lace-up heeled boots on her feet. Her long brown hair bounced off her shoulders as she smiled at me.

I wasn't jealous of Jasmine. She looked beautiful. I just didn't understand why she was allowed to be, while my own wings were clipped by Todd. I was wearing an old sweater, a pair of jeans, and sneakers. My pregnant body hidden; my hair scraped back into a bun. I was a shadow of myself. I used to be Jasmine and now I was pale and invisible.

'What did you get?' she asked, pointing at my shopping bag. I pulled out the pink and black lacy bra and showed her, along with the matching underwear, the only fragment left of who I was once. I wanted to tell her, we would have been friends when I used to be me.

'Congratulations,' she said, pointing at my stomach. 'Todd told me.'

'Thank you.'

On the way home, Todd pulls the bag off me.

'Slut underwear, again.'

The fights became worse. Todd made friends with more beautiful young women. I couldn't keep track of them all. They had tiny toned bodies and I felt ugly and afraid of my own changing body. Todd would take them out for coffee, spend hours answering their late-night phone calls. The pregnancy hormones made me sad; a deep, intense sadness I'd never felt before. I'd cry constantly. Mostly when I saw couples wheeling their child in a pram, looking happy and normal.

One afternoon, I crawl into bed and I can't get up. I'm lying on the mattress, staring out the window. Todd walks in and shakes me by the shoulders.

'Get up,' he says.

'I can't.'

'You can. Get up.'

I roll away from him and curl further into the doona. I want Todd to climb into bed with me, put his arms around my stomach and make me feel less alone. I also want to defy him.

'You are such a fucking loser, Rita. You are so pathetic.' I start to cry and as I'm wiping my face, he starts laughing. My bed is positioned by a window, and I think to myself, if I took three steps, all of this would be over. I could just float away from here.

I hear the sound of his footsteps as they walk away from me, the door closing behind him. I don't know how much time I have but I begin to move, finally. I call Peter.

'You need to come and get me.'

I throw my things in the back of Peter's car, shaking the whole drive to his house. My phone lights up, again and again. Todd has come home to find our bedroom bare and my side of the wardrobe empty.

I wanted to be a mother very badly. Sitting at my best friend's house, I would stare at a Post-it note stuck to the corner of my laptop. It had the number for the abortion clinic at the Royal Women's Hospital. I thought about how Todd would be an omnipotent force in the life of my child, one that would undermine any of the safety and love I could provide. I would be unable to stop him. He would be a hurricane that would blow me through court hearings and custody battles. I would be sending a child off with a packed lunch into a car with a man I couldn't trust to be sober, or speak with kindness. I could still be a mother, but if it meant a lifetime of being tethered to Todd, it wasn't the motherhood I wanted.

One night I saw a photo on his Instagram of one of the pretty, blonde girls I'd seen passing through the house. Pregnancy hormones make you feel like the hulk. I felt like that all the way through unlocking the door, walking up the stairs and entering the bedroom where Todd was passed out drunk in bed. I felt that way when I saw a tangle of blonde hair and a star-patterned bra lying in the bed with him. I felt that way when I went through his wallet, took a few hundred dollars, stole his cigarettes, and then pilfered what I could from the unknown blonde's handbag. I felt that way when she woke up and saw me hunched in the corner like some kind of pregnant gremlin, rifling through drawers and cupboards.

'I'm so sorry, Rita.' I recognised her. I'd been for coffee with her too.

That afternoon, I rang the number on the Post-it. I went in for my ultrasound and saw my baby for the first time on the screen. I'm sorry, I thought. I sat there in my hospital room, a thick sanitary pad between my legs to capture all the blood that would leak from me after my baby was removed from me. My phone beeped, again and again. I look down and it's from Todd. There are photos of me naked, sucking his dick, videos of us fucking.

'I'll show everyone,' it said.

I close my phone. I let the nurse put me onto a bed and wheel me into the operating theatre. As they come towards me with the gas mask, I start to panic. Suddenly the resolve I had has gone and I want to run. I begin to claw at the sides of the bed, I start screaming.

'I've changed my mind,' I'm trying to say, but all that's coming out is gurgling noises and half sobs.

The doctor looks bored, but the nurse next to me takes my hand and holds it in hers. She tells me to look at her and she says something soothing, and while I'm not looking, they slide a needle into my hand.

I wake up in a La-Z-Boy recliner. There's a packet of sweet biscuits and a cup of tea in front of me. It is silent except for the sound of the clock ticking. I can feel a sharp pain between my legs and a sticky wetness. I start crying, hunched over and sobbing on the seat and I cry out for somebody to bring my mum in. She rushes in. Just before she embraces me, I see something pass over her face. It's relief.

RL Grimes Halloween Mix 2013

The first time I took proper drugs was with Nicole and Peter. We got three ecstasy pills from Nicole's boyfriend, who worked as the manager at the local KFC. We waited until Nicole's mum went out and dropped them in her lounge room. An hour goes past and the three of us are standing there.

'Can you feel anything?' Peter says.

'Not really. Maybe?'

'This is taking too long,' says Nicole. She pours us each a shot of tequila and begins packing a bong. 'Maybe this will help.'

The pills kick in as soon as we take a hit from the bong. Peter's trying to pull the treadmill down from where it's resting on the wall, saying he really wants to go for a run. My hands feel like somebody else's. Nicole vomits tequila all over the floor and crawls to the space where the door meets the patio so she can keep her legs warm and face cool. We all lose track of time and space.

'Peter?' I'm walking around the house. I find my brother in Nicole's bedroom, the doona pulled up to just under his eyes. He peeps over at me, watching the tiny television in her room.

I get into the bed and sit next to him. He's watching SBS News. We want to change the channel but we can't.

'Peter?'

'Yeah?'

'How long is this going to last?'

My brother pulls himself together and gives me a squeeze on the hand.

'It will end soon. Don't worry.'

We go back to watching the tiny television, with its images of suicide bombings, climate change, hurricanes and stock market crashes.

———

The second time, I'm in a serviced apartment. I lean down to the table. I feel my heart pounding in my chest. I take the $50 note, roll it into a small tube and block one nostril like Sarah showed me. I lean in and sniff the line of MDMA.

'Wow,' I say, 'this is way better than how I remembered it.'

'This is pure stuff,' she says, 'it's totally different.'

I go outside to the balcony and there stands a tall, tattooed guy in a white singlet. He hands me a lighter as his teeth grind together, the setting sun reflecting off his Ray-Bans.

'Thanks,' I say. Years later, we'll bump into each other at a Crystal Meth Anonymous meeting in Prahran and go for a coffee, smoking cigarettes, and I'll say, *isn't that weird that you were there the first time?*

———

Josh sees me standing at the bar. I'm leaning over to get a cocktail napkin, and he's mixing a negroni. I wave to him. He smiles but then his face drops and he races towards me and throws the drink over my head.

'What the fuck!'

'Your HAIR was on fucking FIRE!'

I sniff. I look down and see the charred remains of my ponytail and the candle it had been sitting in.

I start laughing and so does Josh and I have to sit down because I'm rolling so hard I can't see properly. I snip the crispy ends of my hair off with the scissors used to trim the garnishes for the cocktails.

———

I'm standing in the shower, my eyes rolling into the back of my head. There's another girl in here and we are standing naked together under the shower and I can't stop staring at her giant boobs. I suggested we take a shower together because I'm super high and so is she and we don't do anything. We just stand under the falling water and talk about our childhoods and it feels really, really good.

———

I peel my eyes open. I'm lying on the couch, wrapped in a blanket. My clothes are somewhere in the room. Josh and his friend Damien are lying on the floor, curled under the doona together. I can hear this rhythmic thudding sound. It screeches and hisses, and then there's a slam, with footsteps pounding after it. I sit still, trying to work out what the noise means.

Then the music starts. I recognise it, I used to strip to it a lot. Whitesnake? Warrant? I rack my brain and then I remember. Poison!

I crawl across the couch and open the blinds and I see my neighbour come out; the source of the noise explained. He's throwing open the door of his house and slamming it shut as he walks in figure eights around the communal driveway in our block of units. I reach for my cigarettes and light one as I keep peeping out.

He's a big guy. He starts shouting and screaming. He finishes his lap of the concrete and throws the door open again and then crashes it shut. I flinch and almost burn myself with my cigarette. Am I hallucinating?

'Wake up!' I poke Josh with my foot. I turn to look back out of the window and gasp.

'Oh my fucking FUCK, he's got an axe!'

My neighbour is swinging a woodcutter's axe at the fence like we are in the wilds of Poland and it's the regional strongman contest. Except, I imagine then, they don't scream 'It's time to CLEAN up this NEIGHBOURHOOD' while wearing a sweat-stained wifebeater.

We all peer out the window, transfixed by this maniac. There's enough molly left in our bloodstream to be curious but not enough left to be calm. I'm picturing him chopping through my front door like Jack Torrance in *The Shining* and then I see the red and blue police lights as they make their way down the driveway.

'HIDE EVERYTHING!'

We pick up baggies, bongs, buds of weed and toss them under the kitchen sink as we burn incense and throw open the bathroom windows. My neighbour is thrown to the ground and placed in the lock up of the police wagon, and we try to act like we haven't been high for the last fifteen hours when they knock on the door.

———

It's the Melbourne Show. My friend Thomas and I are at the top of the big dipper. It pauses, to allow for maximum antici-pation before the drop. I hear a *crack* and sniff—I know that smell. Thomas smiles at me as he holds his nostrils over a bottle of Jungle Juice.*

---

*   Amyl nitrate, or 'poppers'.

'Want some?' he says.

I take the bottle, inhale and quickly shove the lid back on.

As the ride begins to plummet I start to scream, and then laugh hysterically and it feels like my brain and face are melting off and going to splatter all over the pavement.

———

I think we've all been awake for about seventeen hours now. We're in my tiny unit in Brunswick, me, my best friend, Josh and his friend. It started off how it was supposed to—taking turns to run hot baths and chain-smoke as we spoke about our trauma and pain. Listening to Boney M. and deep house remixes of Fleetwood Mac, lying on the sheepskin rug with our eyes rolling into the back of our heads. Morning comes and we're all still very high. We move on to red wines and Valiums, but none of us are getting sleepy.

Cut to a few hours later. I'm on the couch, curled into the foetal position, watching mattress infomercials, unable to move. My friends are in various head-cradling positions around the kitchen and bedroom. The shadow people lurk in the corner of our eyes and I keep hallucinating that my cigarette smoke is my dead cat Bing, running out to greet me.

The four of us eventually regroup, try to eat some greasy pizzas I've had delivered. The mood is tense as we individually trip our dicks off and try not to let on to each other about how spooked we are.

'You know what this reminds me of,' says Josh.

'What?'

'This research chemical I tried once. Took a few days to wear off.'

I turn back to the TV. *How good.*

———

The photoshoot wraps and the three of us are in the luxe hotel suite I booked. Josh, my boyfriend at the time, and myself. The photographer leaves the room, picking up his bag and shutting the door. As soon as the door clicks, we lunge for the coffee table, clear it and lay out the goods.

MDMA and a few points of meth. Meth I could take or leave, really. I had no judgement against it, it was just that I mostly didn't feel much when I smoked it. I was awake, I felt like chatting, but I never got the glow my boyfriend or Josh did. It never really clicked for me the way that doing downers (I liked pharmaceutical opioids) or molly did. Amphetamines/methamphetamines were more about keeping me awake while I rolled.

We all get totally cranked. The evening culminates in the usual way—us all lying on top of each other on some soft surface (couch, bed, mountain of blankets on the floor) as we each discuss how much we love each other. Like, REALLY love each other. I would die for you, we all say, passing the crack pipe between us. Sometimes my boyfriend and Josh make out, which I find really hot.

Josh and I took too much Xanax once. One minute we were sitting there, drooling and watching cartoons and the next minute, Josh was all '*Maybe I am bi? I'm so attracted to you.'* We make out and then I gave him a blow job and quite frankly I felt like turning myself into the police the next day as a sex criminal. About halfway through I stopped and I'm like, *Josh, that's so ok if you're bi but I swear to god I feel like I'm blowing my brother.*

So, now just my boyfriend and Josh make out and I watch. They turn to me in the hotel room and my boyfriend says (he has this impregnation fetish that he only ever talks about when we are really, really high): 'You know what would be really sweet? If both Josh and I had sex with you, and came in you, and then you got pregnant and then we would never know who the father was, so we would be a family, and both take care of it.'

For a minute, I was kind of like—*fuck it, why not. That sounds nice.*

——————

When I take MDMA
    I feel loved.
    I am love.
    I'm in love.*

---

*   I am not a current drug user, but I was for a long time. My decision to stop using is not about morality, but simply an incompatibility. I will always support and stand behind the sex workers who are active or former users, and advocate for the decriminalisation and/or legalisation of drug usage.

Bitch, butch, femme

You catch your eyes on your reflection in the mirror on the wall, in the lap dance room. You see a face look back at you as you bring your arms around their shoulders, press the pink sequined fabric around your chest into their face. Who is that woman in the reflection? Two selves intertwine and it leaves you, in the dance room, making a decision that winged eyeliner is now just for work. Because you don't know which self you are looking at right now, which person you are. The song stops and you break out of your trance and ask if he'd like to extend.

———

I cleaned my wardrobe the other day. I sat down and tossed out the jeans that are too big, an act of defiance. I will not allow them to fit me again. I colour coded all the silk slip dresses and stacked the stilettos on a shelf and moved the long, grey cardigan to the 'work' side of the wardrobe; my Dr. Martens boots, my ripped Levi's, flannel shirt, metal band shirts to the other. I have one white turtleneck dress (me) and the matching one in black, that goes to the other side of the wardrobe. I'm frantically trying to create dissonance between the two identities. I make a joke, say it's my Scorpio Rising on one side (me) and the Gemini sun on the colourful, sexy, playful side.

———

When I came out as a sex worker, it wasn't a bold choice I made because I was fearless, proud and unapologetic. I came out because a porno I was in had started circulating among my friendship group and I knew if people smelt blood in the water, they'd attack. I was eighteen, and what I did was deviant, taboo and strange. I decided to come out to save face. To assert control over my own narrative. It worked, sort of. However, sometimes I wonder if I went back in time, denied, left behind the bunch of people who thought watching me naked online was a group bonding activity and simply blurred my face behind a sheet of pixels, just legs and ass and tits visible? Did I make a mistake becoming a face out worker? What would life be like if nobody knew me as Gia, as Tira, as the girl with the dildo in her ass on the internet? Would I still love the things I once did?

———

The first time I ever had sex was with a woman. She was very beautiful. We met on Myspace and became friends, but every time we went for coffee, or shopped together, or watched movies on my bed, I would look over and stare at her. She had long brown hair and it curled around her face and pale blue eyes. I watched and looked for any signals or signs, anything that would tell me it was safe to tell her I thought she was beautiful, funny, interesting.

We had our first kiss on the slide at a playground, because I finally worked up the courage to tell her I liked her. It felt good, natural, to kiss a woman. It was soft.

I had a boldness in me that I look back at in surprise, and I think it was partially due to having Peter, who was unashamed and unapologetic about being gay. I wanted to hold my girlfriend's hand in public, I wanted to be affectionate with her around people. There was always a feeling of fear though, that shadowed my grasp around her waist at a bus stop. The fear somebody would scream out *dyke*, or *lez,* or something else homophobic that you'd hear in the backwater suburbs.

She came from a Catholic family who had no idea I was her lover. I broke my vegetarianism over the steaming hot lasagna her mum placed on the table, with my ingrained sense of politeness and my lust for home-cooked food. At dinner I caught her mother giving me a look, passing me a plate but hesitating before she placed it down. I wasn't surprised. I had a shaved head. I may as well have walked in wearing a GAY PRIDE t-shirt.

I remember the lasagna because after we ate it, we went up to her room and shut the door and got into bed together, under the doona and into each other's arms. We kissed and she took my pants off and put her hand down my underwear and soon I came for the first time.

Eventually we broke up, and lost contact. I grew my hair and dated men exclusively, having queer sex when I was blackout drunk at parties to titillate guys. I reframed having sex for the first time, said it was with the guy in the year above me, in a shed, a painful, emotionally devoid experience. But it's a lie, because it was really with my girlfriend, who I really loved, and it was really good.

————

Being an open sex worker afforded me a lot of opportunities with my art. Because I was open and out, I was able to connect with people.

I started writing a column for a local street magazine, and then articles in other magazines and the whole time, I wrote them under my work name.

I immersed myself in my work persona. I wanted to be feminine and beautiful and sexy and mysterious. I wanted to be the perfect woman. The perfect woman didn't like other women, didn't want to fuck them. I performed my gender and pretended I was straight.

————

My first proper job was at a lingerie store. I was hired as a Christmas casual when I was sixteen. Before that, I'd been toasting sandwiches and making lattes at local coffee shops, but now I had a glamorous job. I worked in a store where all the women had perfect make-up, and my manager did burlesque on the weekend. She was tall and thin, with high cheekbones and jet-black hair swept into a tight bun, the green lace of one of our most expensive sets peeking out from under her work uniform.

I was afraid I wouldn't be hired. A few months prior, Nicole and I had stolen from them. We put bras and panties on under our school dresses and breezed out the front doors, the electronic tags cut out with a pair of nail scissors Nicole kept in her handbag. In the interview for the position, I sweated bullets. I was petrified there was CCTV footage of me, and I kept expecting the manager to reach across the table and slap a pair of cuffs on me.

When I dropped out of Year 11, the lingerie store hired me full time. I woke up every morning with a sense of purpose as I got on the bus to the city, watching everyone trudge past me in their school uniform. When the group email went around, and I saw I was the fifth best salesperson that year, in the whole country, I felt a sense of pride I'd never had before. I was awarded company currency that I could spend on a staff order of lingerie. With fifty per cent off and vouchers, I picked everything, and when it arrived at my door, in a big, brown box, I pawed over every piece.

I had the corsets, the suspender belts, the French lace, the Italian silk and the Swarovski crystals on the bras. You wouldn't have caught me dead in anything that didn't match and without a pair of hold-up stockings on.

———

I open my chest of drawers and arrange my bras, tuck the matching G-strings next to them, with the suspenders, and separate them with tissue paper. The bodysuits, chemises and baby doll nighties are hung on their special little hangers and arranged on my clothes rack.

I'm folding bras on to hangers. I'm the assistant manager now. I keep lollies in the drawer for the other girls and teach them how to sell. A woman walks in and begins browsing so I greet her, and we start to chat, about her outfit, the weather and how good the sales are at the moment.

'Let me know if you get stuck with a size!' I return back to the pile of bras on my workbench.

She comes over.

'I'm actually looking for something kind of specific. Do you have anything that's kind of . . . sexy secretary?'

I take a sideways look at her boobs (you get really good at clocking somebody's cup size when you do it all day long), stack my arms full of black lingerie and pop her in a change room.

'You could do any of these,' I say, as I'm fitting her. 'With you know, like a white shirt, a pencil skirt, some thigh-highs.'

The woman turns and admires herself in the mirror.

I start babbling away about my boyfriend and how I buy lingerie for him.

'Is it like, a dress up thing, for your boyfriend?' I say.

'Sort of.'

'Sort of?'

She turns to me and flicks her long blonde hair.

'I'm an escort, the guy who I'm seeing tonight wants . . . a more secretary vibe.'

'Oh! Wow, I've never met an escort before.'

She starts laughing.

'You have definitely met escorts before, working here. You just didn't know they were.'

I think back to all my selling. The women who'd buy three sets, all our most expensive line, and pay in cash. The girl I had yesterday, with the most spectacular boob job I'd ever seen, a solid 10G that looked incredible in our push-up bra. The girls who'd hold up the sexiest scrap of fabric we had and ask for it in their size. *Oh good,* I'd think, *a fun customer.*

'You'd be good at it,' says the woman, looking at me through the mirror. 'You are really nice. Pretty. Personable.'

I start laughing, but it's not because I think it's an insane idea. I'm actually very flattered.

'I might have to wait,' I reply, 'because I'm seventeen.'

'Wow,' she replies, adjusting the bra. 'You seem much older. If you ever want to start, I know some good agencies. When you are eighteen.'

She buys three sets and writes the name down of an agency on a card. I put it away in my handbag and promptly forget about it.

———

My boyfriend is fucking me and I'm in my Megadeath t-shirt, my cotton underwear pulled to the side.

You wouldn't have caught me dead in anything that didn't match and without a pair of hold-up stockings on.

All my lingerie lies crumpled, in a plastic tub, tossed together. Bra clips snag on the back of lace and old stockings, shredded and torn mingle with new pairs. The tub is shoved at the back of the wardrobe and every time I have a booking, I heave it out and sift through tangles of fabric, grasping at whatever matches and can be tossed on in a hurry. My client asks for stockings and I roll my eyes, irritated at the thought of a suspender belt. I could never wear any of this stuff in my real life. It's tainted, ruined for me.

———

Butch. Femme. Butch. Femme.

I switch between my two personas, constantly feeling torn between the two. I pretend I'm straight online and the difference between my work self and my real self increasingly blurs. Any visible queerness, like my flannel shirt and Dr. Martens, I keep hidden from my Instagram—in case one of my clients sees it, in case it damages my business and my ability to make money.

On dates with women I get wasted and we make out, and sometimes fuck and then I ghost them. I'm a fuckboy. With men, I can play pretend, I can be my work self, I can pull the wool over their eyes. But women—women are perceptive. They'll see the masquerade. She might need me to bring the two halves together and how do I explain that I don't know how to? I don't know how to reconcile this split anymore.

I am alienated from the online queer sex worker community. I look straight. I like the memes and laugh at the jokes but I'm kept at a distance. I look like an infiltrator. I understand. I don't belong with the openly queer sex workers and I don't belong with the heterosexual ones.

I don't know where I belong.

———

In order to go forward, in order to survive, sometimes we have to write our own stories. We need to reframe what happens to us, we need to get up again and do it all over. I stare at my wardrobe and then I come downstairs and open my laptop. I have to edit this book today and I find a story, about my grandmother dying. I forgot she died. I buried it away, because after she died, in her house, with her cup of tea on the side table, I went to work. I need to go to work because I need to go to the other side of my wardrobe. I drink a few glasses of wine and I do my make-up the way

I always do it for work. I put on my heels and my silk slip dress and I go to Crown Towers.

My client pins me down and he fucks me without a condom on and when I realise what is happening, I strike him as hard as I can. I scream and he tells me I'm insane, that he has had the condom on the whole time. I feel like I'm losing my mind, but there it is—in his hand. He waves it at me, in my face. I know what I felt, I think to myself. I know it wasn't there. So you know what I did? I stayed.

When I get home, I can't even cry. I just ring up one of my friends.

'He's pacing around the room, the suite, telling me how he could have been a doctor or a lawyer, because he is so intelligent and worldly. He shows me his Russian girlfriend on his phone, weirdly specific to mention she is Eastern European. He then asks me if I'd had a nose job, because I look like I'd needed one? He puts his business card into my hand.'

My fingers trace the name which is now forever imprinted in my mind, and I tell my friend his name, and she says, *he did the same thing to me.*

I didn't remember any of this until I read the story I wrote, while I was editing this book. I was so disturbed that my mind had taken a memory and hidden it. My memory said, YOUR grandmother died, not HERS. He was inside HER, not YOU.

———

I'm at my therapy session, explaining my wardrobe to my therapist, telling her about the clothes, that I don't like lingerie, that I once did. I told her, I've never had a Bambi moment with high heels like the other baby strippers. I've worn 6-inch heels and higher since I was fifteen. I strapped my feet into the highest pair of stripper heels I could find— clear plastic with a diamanté collar on the ankle—and strode out into the bucks party on my first shift. Where has it gone? Why can't I do these things anymore? Why do I see a stranger's face in the mirror when I put make-up on? Why do I feel so disconnected from my femininity? Am I gay? That doesn't make sense to me, because I like men some- times. Am I living in denial? Am I butch? Am I femme?

I have taken my patience, docility, warmth and my ability to give a shit, all these notions of femininity and thrust them to the side of my wardrobe with the stilettos. Repressing and relegating anger, resentment, fury, then me turning around and back-handing a client on the other side, the butch side, the bitch side, the gay side, the dyke side, the side I forget. It's not my Jungian shadow self, it's not my 'bad' side, it's me. It's who I am at my core, a woman with duality but forced to live in the shadows, afraid of what life and my income would be like if I allowed her out. Gia. Rita. Two sides of the same coin, yet—why do they feel so separate?

I have learnt to take the bad things that happen, and place them on the side of the wardrobe with the lingerie and the heels. All the bad things that have happened, they happened to *her*.

'How do I bring these two sides together?' I say to my therapist.

She looks at the clock on the wall.

'Let's talk about it next week. We are out of time today.'

Love

When people picked up this book, I suppose they wanted to read something glossy and sexy. The salacious tell-all, the glamorous and mysterious life they must think I am living. Being Gia, getting to be a different person. I didn't realise this book would become so inward facing, that in the act of writing about my life I would uncover so many secrets about myself. With each story, I peel back another layer and find a hidden room, a walled-off section of my mind. I feel as though I'm in a labyrinth and each time I get closer to the light, I stumble and trip over debris cluttering the floor. I am forced to examine what prevents me from moving forward, to hold it up and inspect it from every angle.

When I am Gia, I am in control; I am sexy and powerful. I put on my designer shoes with their blood-red soles and I like the way they pinch the sides of my feet, make me teeter towards the waiting taxi, where I slip in and tuck my dress under me. I blow-dry my hair upside down and sit there and curl it in front of my mirror, crouched naked on my towel. These clothes smell like Tom Ford perfume. I have lingerie that costs more than my groceries for the week that I handwash and hang to dry in my apartment. I sit on the floor of my shower and shave my asshole and sweep bronzer over my cheekbones and gloss my lips. I lock my apartment door and inside my Givenchy bag are condoms, lube, more lingerie, a hairbrush, concealer, baby wipes, dildos, butt plugs, cash for a cab, a phone charger, a portable speaker. The bag was a present from a pay pig, my Louboutins my birthday present from a long-term lover. I love being a whore. I love cheese plates, French champagne and oysters. I like hotel sheets and tiny toiletries and wiping my lubed-up pussy clean on Egyptian cotton hand towels.

I love fucking. I like fucking old men, younger guys, big guys, small guys. I like to look at myself in the mirror above the bathroom sink as some stranger does me from behind and I like to position my head on the pillow just so, in front of the brothel mirrors, and watch myself. I look like a fucking porn star, I think, running my tongue over my lips. I like to fuck strangers because strangers fall in love with me and shower me with compliments, they make me feel desired and special and wanted and they even give me money to be in my presence. I think, I'm worth something.

I know how to love, don't I? I understand the physicality of it, the body language, the way to cock your head, the act of withstanding and enduring. Love is a marathon sprint; love is being hit from every angle and standing steadfast. I stand in front of the mirror before I leave and I'm scowling at myself, pinching my stomach. I feel grotesque, pinching my flesh and imagining how much more money I could make if I lipo'd all the fat from my stomach. My value is directly correlated with my physical appearance and sometimes my thoughts turn dark and stormy as I sit in the Uber on the way to my booking. I'm exhausted. I catch myself in the reflection of the hotel doors, my mouth downturned. I breathe in, and force myself to smile, shake my head and I keep that smile there. Even when they are rude, even when I'm not good enough.

———

I've met somebody. I've met him properly now. He walked into my apartment, tall and handsome, so different from the friend I've known all these years. I looked up from what I was doing and I realised I'd never seen how great his smile was. It lit up his face and I felt my own change, unforced.

They always said to me, oh Rita, it will happen when you aren't looking. I always thought that was the weirdest advice ever, like we live in a society that doesn't use smartphones to link you up with other single people. As if you could somehow organically meet a lover. As if my life would play out like a romantic comedy and I'd have a meet-cute in the supermarket where we'd both reach for the same eggplant and boom, fall in love. What kind of fucking dumb advice is that? Have you noticed the people that tell you that are always people who are happily coupled up after meeting each other at like, a law firm, where they both have great jobs, no history of mental illness and a sexual appetite that's been whetted by Catholicism and authoritarian parenting? I'm good thanks, I say, logging back into the kink dating app I've downloaded. Later one night I met a guy from there, and he told me he's never had sex without a condom on—ever. He tried to tell me his #MeToo story about the time his long-term girlfriend got on his dick raw (I imagine after years of using condoms, she'd had enough) and I'm like, dude, do you have a germ phobia? He ended up cable-tying me to a chair and we had a good time but maybe everyone was right. Maybe I was looking too hard in all the wrong places.

I'm standing in my bedroom and posing in my underwear in front of my mirror. Post the photo to my Instagram story and this guy slides in. It's been a bleak, never-ending tundra of messages from sunburnt guys holding up fish, tattooists with girlfriends and male submissives and finally I snap. I've given up. I accept my lot in life. Cock cages and shooing away cheaters. *Maybe I should give this fishing dude a go*, I think. *That boat looks expensive.*

So I'm in my lounge room and there's my friend and he's here because he replied to my post and said, *I'll choke you.*

I'm looking at his handsome face and the curls at the nape of his neck that I twist with my fingers as I straddle his lap. I want to be choked and he wants to choke me, but we are too busy talking. We are too busy seeing each other properly. I see his broad shoulders and his charisma and his deep laugh and the astute observations he makes. I see his intelligence and his wit and I'm so shocked that he's been standing there for seven years and I didn't notice.

We get into bed and leave the salt lamp on, bathing the room in soft pink light.

'Oooooh,' he says, 'this your magic healing lamp ionising the air, is it?' He is a sceptic and doesn't try to hide his laughter at me trying to work out his birth chart on Co-Star. We start to fuck. He's got his hands around my throat and then it slows down as he kisses me and then we make love, and his body leans on top of mine, wrapping his arms around me. I look up at his eyes and they reflect mine and then I break it by saying, *what's with this weird Christian sex*, when I want to say, *I love you*.

———

We are just dating at this stage, and when I get in the car, he asks what I did that day.

'I saw a psychic, and then came home, cleaned the house, got ready to meet you.'

'Oh, you aren't getting away that easily. Tell me about the psychic.'

'I know you don't believe in these things. Let's not.'

'I'm open to it. Tell me.'

So I tell him, my hands in my lap. I don't tell him I asked the psychic about him, and she roared with laughter and clapped my hands in hers and said, you have nothing to worry about. You two will be great together.

'You know,' he says, 'this is all psychoanalysis and cold reading, right? That it's all just her giving you leading questions?'

He goes on and on, and I stop listening. I'm looking out of the window, and remembering how it felt to touch Peter's warm, living hands again when I meditated with the psychic. The last time I touched it, his hand, they had laid it out of the casket, the rest of him covered with a sheet. His body had deteriorated so badly when they found him in the motel room, his hand was all they could salvage.

I stay quiet through dinner and the ride home because I am afraid to tell people when they hurt me. I am passive, afraid they will leave me, see that I am too much work. I have been conditioned by myself and others to believe I am always at fault, my emotions toxic, my feelings nonsensical. I have downed a whole bottle of white wine to block out the feeling that he is right, that death has come and swept my brother to a place where he will never speak or have warm hands. Wine usually works at shutting my mind up, making me quiet and docile, but not tonight. I just remember that I began to yell, told him he could never understand real pain, never know what loss could be and how it feels to have half of you gone. Or maybe I don't. I don't give myself much space for anger.

He gets up and leaves. I slam the bathroom door shut and cry into my hands. I have become an expert at pushing people away before they get too close. I am hyper-vigilant, waiting for the wrong word, the answer I don't want but need so I can begin the work of removing them from my heart. I love the block button. I love exiling my emotions and the people I once cared about to the ends of my psychological earth. I can't explain to him yet that I am in love, terrified that he will leave me, that I have experienced so much loss and pain now I don't know whether I can stand any more, because that would make me sound insane.

I text him from the bathroom. Something is different here because I feel genuinely distressed at the idea that I'm self-sabotaging. I want to do things differently. I quickly type out a message, wiping my eyes with the back of my hands. I get a response immediately. He's just in his car, sitting there. I race downstairs and climb in the passenger seat and say I'm sorry. He grabs my hands and makes me look him in the eye.

'I know that you like that I'm blunt and forward, but I say the wrong things sometimes and you need to tell me. If you tell me, I'll apologise.'

I've never had somebody say that to me before, give me the space to speak up. I have spent most of my life learning how to tell white lies. My need for privacy, validation, space and boundaries have been secondary to that of my family, and subsequently, in my relationships as I grew older. It was partially my fault as well, for never speaking up until it was too late. I thought I had a long fuse and a quick temper. I thought love was when you stood still and let the words wash over you, and that if I had enough strength and a centre that was solid I could let them go. I thought if I couldn't, the only way out was the block button or a string of words that were aimed to kill.

My silence was an open, festering wound and he showed me I could start to heal it by using my voice.

———

He takes me to pick up my cat from my brother's house because I've been away and when we get her, she claws her way out of the cardboard box. I panic but he is red in the face from laughing. She crawls under his seat in the car while I have an anxiety attack.

'I'm so sorry, I'm so fucking weird,' I say, breathing sharply as I try to control the pounding in my chest.

'You are just stressed because all your things aren't in the house. As soon as we get home, you'll be ok.'

He is so calm, all the time.

He unpacks all the groceries; he sets up the cat's food and water bowls. We go out for dinner to a fancy steak restaurant and there he sits, in his work boots and gym shorts and curly hair peeking out the back of his cap.

'I love my bogan wife,' he says to me as I try to surreptitiously vape into my Louis Vuitton handbag on the balcony dining area.

'Say that again,' I place a hand to my ear. I'm half joking. I want to hear it, make sure I didn't mishear him, make sure I'm sure before I say it back.

'I love my bogan wife.'

'One more time . . .'

'I love you.'

The smile isn't forced. I'm not Gia and this isn't a stranger, telling me something intimate I don't want to hear. A token of affection for a woman who doesn't exist, a woman I believe is the better version of myself.

I am loved. He said it first. I try to look back but I can't because I feel so overwhelmed with happiness that I can only stare at my hands and the linen napkins.

———

The labyrinth finally has a purpose. It is learning to be loved. My partner has the task of helping guide me out and there are days where I feel like giving up. So many turns, so many puzzles to work out. I want to stay in the darkness and rest because I am so tired. There are obstacles everywhere for him, land mines. I have so many defences up.

He fucks me in the kitchen, my pyjama pants around my ankles. I can see myself in the reflection. I don't feel like a porn star. I feel scared, like my skin is being turned inside out. I feel like I want to run, very fast, from this love that is being given to me. All I wanted since we started dating was to hear 'I love you,' but now I feel afraid and like shoving the words back in our mouths. I am afraid that I am not capable of giving it back.

My boyfriend asks me if I'm going to come.

'You can just kinda use me if you want, like a fuck doll, you know?'

He comes and instead of crawling on top of him like I usually do, I run to the bathroom and sit and stare at the wall. Then I go downstairs and wrap myself in the blanket on the couch. I sit there and I think to myself, I wish I could cry. I feel like a failure, a professional at fucking who doesn't know how to. He comes downstairs to find me huddled on the couch.

'I am not your client,' he says, holding me. 'I'm not a horny idiot who needs you to fuck me when you don't want to. You don't need to do anything. I don't care if we only have sex once a month. I just want you to be happy.'

I crave my whore life. The anonymous, meaningless and pounding sex where I can be outside my body and it doesn't matter. It just feels good. My feet stuffed into thousand-dollar high heels instead of barefoot on the kitchen tiles. Falling for married men, their wife the barrier preventing us ever doing anything besides hook up. Hotel key cards and a blur applied to the lens. I want the mask of Nars Sheer Glow on my skin and my Uber driver waiting to take me home. I can't tell him it's easier for me to come with strangers. I don't want to submit to this ordeal of being known, of being understood, of being seen. I'm scared to be myself.

———

I have taken care of myself for a long time. I live alone so that when the outside world becomes too much, I can be ugly and imperfect. I can scream, cry, be aggressive. I can be a child inside my own four walls and soothe myself when I throw a tantrum.

Suddenly there is a stranger in my house, and he can see when I'm starting to crumble. Take-away bags in my cupboard that I'm going to put in the recycling bin, soon. The cat's litter needs to be changed. There are empty wine bottles next to the bin and a laundry pile. Gone is the girl in the diamanté G-string on the Instagram story, replaced by stained pyjama pants and greasy hair. I'm furious the veneer is being lifted and ashamed to be seen as human. *He will leave me* my mind plays on repeat. When I got this bad in the past, Peter would come over and put on music and wash all my dishes and vacuum the floor, and fill my prescriptions and place them on the Ajax-wiped bathroom sink. Without Peter, I wait for the storm to pass and the will to keep going to enter my body again. But now I have this stranger here and he's throwing out my Uber Eats bags and bringing me coffee.

I'm finally learning to speak and my partner is teaching me. I throw tantrums, I enact long silences that he refuses to indulge, forcing me to tell him what's wrong so we can work it out. The further into our relationship we go, the more I realise that under everything is a scared child who believes she is defective and unlovable. It's a monumental task but my partner takes it in his stride. I begin to catch myself stomping my feet and then I start to laugh along with him, at the ridiculousness of it all.

———

I have stopped eating, except for a small meal at night. I am hungry all the time, but it makes me feel in control again. In control of something, while I'm pouring my pain and sadness into this book, this book I want so badly to convey a sense of meaning to somebody, to resonate. I cannot control that, so instead I control my food again. My jeans become too big. What a relief. My boyfriend says he can feel my ribs. I am proud. He is not.

I'm standing in JB Hi-Fi. The scales are on the very top shelf and I need the sales assistant to bring them down to me. I watch as she climbs down, the dusty box in her hand.

I walk home, embarrassed that people can see me holding the scales. I wonder what they think. Do they think, look at that fat bitch? Or do they think, she takes care of herself? Taking 'care,' self-surveillance, being a responsible,

functioning citizen in an individualistic, capitalist society.*
Am I taking up as little space as possible? Am I embodying
virtues within my body—is it respectable, tidy, small? Or
am I deviant?

When I stand on the scales I start screaming. When
I drunkenly weighed myself at a booking however long ago,
the number was smaller. I felt elated then. I look back at the
photos I took in lingerie in the bathroom, look at my body,
cry. Is it the same? Am I different?

My boyfriend walks in the door to find me sitting on
the couch, staring at the scales, my mortal enemy. They lift
me up and they bring me crashing down. I have an app on
my phone they send the number to. He's hugging me and
trying to explain to me that if I do it every day, if I eat a little
more, if I try, I can see the number will stay the same. That
I don't need to be so afraid of food, that I can have a life not
dictated by calories and counting and hunger.

'You need to get on them to stop being so afraid.'

———

I walk into the TV unit for what feels like the tenth time
that week.

'God, this fucking THING,' I say, rubbing my knee.

* I remember this concept from reading Foucault at university and
  it has always come to mind whenever I feel myself having those
  thoughts.

My partner looks up from the kitchen table, wedged between my old sofa and an unused cat scratching-post. She prefers the sides of my legs or the arms of the couch.

He looks over at the enormous unit. His giant frame has to move like a Tetris block around my tiny studio apartment. Just a lounge room with a kitchen tacked on the end, and a rickety flight of stairs that leads to a bed above it.

'I didn't want to say it, but . . . I kinda hate that thing.'

I look over at it. I bought it at IKEA years before I understood about functionality or the advantages of owning a measuring tape. I realise I hate it too. I bought it after Peter died, along with my couch. Both oversize remnants from years of having housemates (or well-meaning friends who lived with me while I grieved). I walk up the stairs and see the plastic tub I keep all my lingerie in, the clothes I shoved on top spilling out.

'I think I want new furniture,' I say.

We begin the task of dismantling and rebuilding. We get rid of the oversized furniture. I clean out my cupboards. I rearrange the kitchen. I change the apartment to accommodate us, two people. He stays up until three in the morning to put together a chest of wooden drawers for me.

I feel the walls come down as I watch him, hunched over the pieces with a power drill. I get up and walk over and put my hands around his waist and cry.

'What's wrong?' he says, pulling me into him.

'I never thought I would have this,' I say. 'I never thought I'd be happy. I never thought I wouldn't have to compromise. I never thought somebody would love me with the sex work, the trauma, that somebody would do anything like this for me.'

I never thought somebody would want to build a home with me. There it is, I thought to myself. This is love.

———

We drive straight down the Hume Highway from Newcastle to Sydney. I fall asleep at one point, keeping my hand in yours. I go through every playlist, picking all the songs as the road stretches ahead of us. I find all my songs, all the music and albums that others have ruined for me.

I dedicate them to you now.

SONGS FOR YOU
Playground Love—Air
Hallelujah—Leonard Cohen
Lay Lady Lay—Bob Dylan
I Walk the Line—Johnny Cash
Burning Love—Elvis Presley
Cruisin'—Smokey Robinson

DEATH

Sober

I am flying 20,000 feet above sprawling salt plains, to the centre of Australia—Alice Springs. A client, who we shall refer to as 'D,' has asked me to accompany him for three days. I am dressed inconspicuously but the miners seated in the rows in front of me keep peering over. I am somewhat of an oddity on this flight, the heavy ink on my arms in stark contrast to the white of my dress.

As I disembark the plane, the hot winds whip my dress around me and I see him standing at the gate, dressed in R.M. Williams from head to steel-capped boots. D and I walk over to the luggage carousel. His hand is on the small of my back, but his disinterest in my arrival is what's turning me on. There's nothing I enjoy more than a sadistic, emotionally detached dominant.

Inside my luggage is the following—one flogger, three canes, two packets of bondage tape, a package of six black plastic-coated pegs, two weighted nipple/labia clamps, a shark jaw gag, a Hitachi magic wand and two glass butt plugs. All purchased with D's American Express card and shipped to me, at his request.

He walks me out to the car, and I drink in the scenery as we make the drive from the airport. Blue skies roll into the red earth. Huge mountain ranges line the road either side, with the grey flowers of the gum tree the only litter.

We arrive at The Hilton in Alice Springs. It's a relic of years gone by, a monstrosity from the 1970s, complete with an old gym that has faded aerobics posters on the walls, and the smell of acrid sweat clinging to the workout mats. The pool is an enormous hexagon and surrounded by empty sun loungers. Wood panelling and linoleum and lodge style furnishings complete my Kubrick fantasy.

The check-in clerk stares at the two of us.

'So, it's just the room with the . . . queen, correct?'

'Yes,' D answers, looking annoyed. He adjusts his hearing aid, the liver spots on the back of his hands visible next to the cuff of his shirt.

Right, I imagine the receptionist clerk thinking, *not going to touch that one with a ten-foot pole.*

We get in the elevator to go to our room and a couple smiles at us.

'Is this your granddaughter?' the woman says.

In the safety of the room he places my bags down, kisses me, hands me a key card and leaves. He's here on a conference for a few days. I can do whatever I like with my day, so long as by 5 p.m. I'm ready to have the living daylights beaten out of me.

The silence of the room is broken by the hum of cicadas and lawnmowers as I open the balcony doors. The hot air rushes over me. There is a bottle of champagne chilling in an ice bucket. I pour a large glass, light a cigarette and wonder what I'm going to do with my day.

I shower, do my make-up, arrange the sex toys, slip my feet into the 7-inch stripper heels I brought with me. I take a bunch of selfies, rearrange the room, listen to INXS on my speakers, and get gradually more and more wasted as I wait for him to return.

He comes back with a second bottle of champagne. I am kneeling on the ground at his feet as he strokes my head like a cat. 'You are feeling submissive, aren't you?' he says to me, cupping my chin in his hand. I have a good buzz going by now. I crawl over to the bed and position myself on all fours.

If I really thought about it, I don't know if I like pain so much as I like taking it to make another person feel pleasure. D casually remarks about another girl who subbed for him, who let him cane her to the point they accidentally drew blood. I feel inadequate already and it fills me that I possess an inability to please. I'm going to try harder this time.

D is very good with a cane—light taps, then heavier blows. My eyes are rolling into the back of my head from the feeling of his palms caressing my bruised skin. The room is beginning to spin. Thank god—finally I feel something. I feel the buzz sweep over me, its intoxicating embrace better than any orgasm, any memory. I am finally numb, taken away but also more present than ever.

The next thing I feel is D's hard-on pressing against my black and blue flesh, then inside me. He is fucking me rhythmically, but something doesn't feel right. I don't remember him putting a condom on. I freeze. My brain is locked in submissive mode, unable to say, 'stop.' I don't want him inside me and I didn't ask him to do this but I feel completely powerless. I'm so deep into sub-space, so alone in this town, trapped in a hotel room. I am here for two more days. I can't make a scene.

I feel him groan and go flat against my body, as I continue to kneel, frozen. I reach behind myself and feel for the latex barrier, but it's not there.

'Where's the condom? What the fuck?'

'I'm sorry,' he says. 'I got carried away.'

'Carried away?'

'It won't happen again. I'm a little drunk, I apologise. Don't spoil the holiday.'

I start to feel panic take over me. I want to cry, throw up, scream. I need to smooth this over now though, because we've got another 48 hours together. I go silent, drain the rest of my glass, place a pillow in between us and roll over to sleep. I hear him beginning to snore, and I reach for my phone and open Google search.

I think it might be time to go to AA.

———

AA had been lurking on my periphery for some time. It seemed like the place I might need to go at some point. I'd been putting it on the wait-list, like something I'd check off later on, when I got to rock bottom. What happened in Alice Springs tipped the scales. Something inside me clicked. I felt out of control. I was back in that room with the pale blue eyes, the piss running down my throat, the tear in my ass.

———

So there I am, my fingers slick with grease from the fries I am shovelling into my mouth in the back of the cab. I can feel them spilling out and dropping into my lap, coating the wine stains on my shirt with salty crumbs. The driver pulls over and lets me out. He speeds away before I realise I'm in the wrong place. I'm in Kings Cross, miles from where I'm meant to be.

I light a cigarette, teetering on my heels. The wind is cold, and I huddle into my jacket as I begin the trek for another taxi. It's dark, and I think of my friends back at the wine bar. I wonder if they noticed my abrupt exit, the rush to get to the toilet, its cool ceramic bowl soothing my aching forehead. I can barely see, but I can make out car lights ahead of me. In my hand is a bottle of red wine I'm taking to my friend's house for after drinks-drinks. As I stand in the middle of the road to flag down the car and it draws closer, I realise it's a cop car. Fuck shit, I stand back and try to look sober. It drives slowly past me and I stumble backwards.

I think to myself, *I should totally post this on my work escort account.* Send tweet.

I am horny. I am lonely. The wine isn't working like it normally does. Instead of dragging me back into my skin, I am viewing myself from afar. I am anaesthetised, constantly. Standing under the burning lights of the Coca-Cola sign in the Cross, I realise that this is my rock bottom. It feels anti-climactic.

———

'This is my first day of sobriety,' I said. The group paused for a moment, all eyes turned to me, and a murmur of congratulations went around the room. People shared their stories and the meeting wrapped up with a serenity prayer and I was ejected back out into the real world, terrifyingly sober and alone. 'Keep coming back,' people said to me, telling me about the power of '90 meetings in 90 days'. So I do. I keep coming back, first to meetings in Sydney on my escort tour, and then to meetings in Brisbane where I am living now. It is here that I realise why I've been drinking for so long, and so heavily. I'm really fucking sad and scared and I don't know who the fuck I am.

Was I an alcoholic? No.

Did I have a drinking problem? Yes.

Was it my fault I was raped (both times) because I was drunk? No. It took me a long time to stop blaming myself for that.

———

So this was the redemptive narrative arc. I got sober, I left my boyfriend, I started a new life. I went to therapy, I got medicated, I started making my zines, I bought house plants. Still a hooker but a good hooker, right? The one who's in AA, not the one snorting lines off dudes' dicks and blowing all her money on tiny designer handbags while on a Xanax shopping spree, or getting day drunk on Moët, letting the morning sun beat down on her shoulders while she stands in the smoking area, kicking her heels off and feeling the astroturf between her toes. It's ok now, because I'm not a fuck up anymore—and it all ends happily. This is what you wanted, right?

———

I'm sitting on the train, and the phone rings. It's Peter. I don't answer because the carriage is packed, but I text him.

'What's up?' I type. 'Just on the train.'

The moving dots are there and then they stop. A moment passes and they start again.

'Just wanted to chat. Speak later.'

———

My friend is holding me. I'm screaming. Just screaming, buckled to the floor. Peter is dead. They found him in a hotel room, a syringe in his arm.

BFF

My first best friend and I met on the floor of a prep classroom, two six year olds who were both Geminis. Her birthday was three days after mine and this felt like a sign we were meant to be best friends. We were inseparable, bonding over our mutual love of Barbies. She had a limited edition, Chinese New Year Barbie which was kept in a box on her top shelf, and we would carefully take it out and move the red dress so it flowed onto the carpet, trailing behind her. Her family moved to the country when we started Year 2, and I sobbed at home, unable to think that anyone would ever be able to fill the void she left behind. I felt understood, seen, heard by her.

Nicole and I met on the monkey bars a couple of months after May moved away. We spent the next eleven years going through every rite of passage together. The first prank call to unsuspecting locals; the first time we sucked in helium and spoke in high-pitched giggles; the first time we stuffed some pot into a cigarette paper and smoked it; the first time we took ecstasy; the first time we shoplifted; the first time we tried to work out what a blow job was and how to give one. Nicole had sex first, explaining it all to me so I was ready when I fucked some guy in the year above me in his shed a few weeks later.

Standing out the front of Lounge on Swanston Street, trying to look like adults as we shivered in the winter fog in our dresses and heels. Both of us clutching our hole-punched learners' permits, borrowed from older women who'd moved onto a full licence. If it was dark and you didn't stare too hard at the identity cards, they sort of looked like us. Buying vodka and lemonades and dancing in our stolen clothes, the pink lights and smoke machine whirling at our feet. The time I tried to kill myself and Nicole called me crying, telling me she would never forgive me if I left her all alone. Smoking bongs and taking the bus to the nail salon instead of Year 10 history. The smell of monomer mixing with the quick dry spray, Nicole's eyes are slowly shutting and flying open as she floats in and out of consciousness, while her French nails are backfilled. This was the time when Rihanna started getting her nails long, pointy and jet black so I watch as the nail tech carefully paints on another layer of black polish, gazing in stoned fascination at the brush strokes on my talons.

I was at Nicole's house, chopping up and packing a bong. I took one hit and I felt the room zoom out and I was suddenly very small, like a tiny toy figurine inside a doll house. I felt my heart seize up and my stomach run ice cold.

'Dude, I don't feel so good,' I said. I then proceeded to have a panic attack as I processed the sheer vastness of reality, space and time, and also that I needed to remember to breathe in case my brain forgot. When it finally wore off, I sat there, staring at the bong. I felt betrayed. Smoking weed had always stifled my depression and quelled my anxiety.

I tried a few more times. I did what all stoners tell you— try this strain, smoke it in a joint, try edibles. But each time I would trip out further and further until I decided I couldn't smoke anymore.

When I think of love, the first place I remember feeling it was when May left and I cried. Another was when I realised one of the glues that bound Nicole and me together was coming unstuck. These were the times I truly felt my heart break. When the dust settles on the end of a romance, is it the best friend we actually miss? For me it was the person who made me laugh, the person who'd say *I love this* when I put on a song, and then hold my hand in the car. The person I partied with, the person I cried with, the person whose tastes differed from mine and the person who'd made you feel seen, heard, understood. Sometimes I'd lose myself in a memory of the sex I'd had with an ex-lover as somebody new touched me, but what I'd think about most was that I missed the friend I once had in my lover.

I have grieved harder for losing a friend than any other connection with a human. After experiencing so much death, I find it preferable—at least you can't check their Instagram and see that they've moved on with a new you, a new friend. I can look back at my ex partners and think, *what the FUCK was I doing?* When I see an old friend, I think *what the fuck are you DOING? Who are you dating? What's new in your life? What are you thinking about?* And mostly, I think about all the things I want to tell them. The guy I'm seeing, my bad day at work, the thing they would find so funny. Then we could just go back to how things were, when we were soulmates.

Best Friends Forever.

The idea that one friend will be the 'best', the closest, has echoed through my life, as it echoes through the lives of many women. When I pull apart this idea and examine it as an adult, I wonder if I've made the healthiest decisions. I wonder if I've placed too much emphasis on one woman being my rock, and if my expectations for 24/7 support, love and understanding are unfair. I think they are. I have felt deficient and grossly incompetent when I've lost close female friendships. I have felt my heart break in ways that were deeper and darker than any other relationship ending. I've been unable to shake the feeling of shame—that people would see my revolving door of BFFs and judge me. I have felt unable to sustain these friendships, but wonder if they were ever sustainable—at full throttle, ride or die, five hours on the phone a day.

I have gone through major periods of my adult life proclaiming I was single, but the truth is there was always a BFF filling the void for me. I was tired of this list of criteria I needed to meet before I was able to be loved, a list that changed like the wind. I wanted a woman to be there on the other end of the phone and say the right things instead of the wrong things. I was chasing unconditional love and I would never be able to get it from my friends because that wasn't their job. I cried because I realised what I thought were soulmates were people who just accepted me in my whole, imperfect form. The fog cleared and I saw it all clearly. I wanted a mother. I wanted a carer. Someone who would take me without judgement or criticism. It was a mother I had searched for all these years in these erratic, unstable, beautiful, intense and *I would die for you* friendships.

Peter answered my collect calls when I missed the last bus home. He was the one who lent me $20 when I was broke so I could buy cigarettes and a coffee after school. He was the one who held my hand in the psych ward, the time I tried to die. He was the one who consoled me when my heart had been broken. He was the one who always picked up the phone, who picked me up from parties, whose home I came to when the world felt dangerous and dark. He was the one who showed me how to do my make-up, he was the one who bleached my hair in the bathroom sink. He was the one who saw me, imperfect and whole, and he loved me. I scream at people that they can never understand what I've lost, but I truly couldn't until that moment either. I had lost my brother, my best friend and I had lost my mother, my parent, my guardian and my tether to this world.

Stripper

The Pink Flamingo is a dive. The winter I started working there, there was no heating. Instead, we had gas bottle, standalone heaters like you'd have at a pub, scattered around the strip club. In the changing room, there was a single heater that you'd crouch in front of to get dressed, your fingers shaking from the cold as you tried to do up the string of your bikini.

Inside the club, there was one large stage. Pink and silver metallic cellophane curtains framed the back wall, and there were technicolour lights that danced across the scratched and grimy stage floor. If you did floor work and writhed on the stage, you'd end up with dirty knees and a dusty ass crack.

The longer you worked at Pinks, the more you understood the terrain of the stained carpet that covered the floors.

Undetectable to the naked eye, lumps in the carpet were at various points across the section from the bar to the toilets. One wrong step and your 8-inch stripper heel would catch, and you'd be sent flying, face first to the ground.

Pinks had a fully stocked bar with neon lights, and haphazard Tiki decorations, and surrounding the bar were huge, squashy red velvet couches. They were shaped in horseshoes around the stage. Under the lights they looked luxurious and retro. When the lights went on at 3 a.m., when the club closed, you could see various suspicious stains and slashes in the upholstery.

To the left of the bar was the Versace room, so named by us, the girls working there. Ornate and lacking in any kind of taste, black satin was staple gunned to the walls and zebra-print throw pillows adorned the black and gold couches. It smelt like stale cigarettes and the floor was sticky from spilt Jack and Cokes.

Yeah, the Pink Flamingo was a shithole. But it was my shithole.

———

It was June when I came back to live with my dad in Melbourne after Peter died. I was living in the old bedroom I'd had when I was a teenager. I'd dyed my hair black from a packet at 1 a.m.

I had to come home. Each morning I would wake up in the warehouse I was living in and, for a second, I would forget that Peter had died. I'd lie there and suddenly it'd hit me that I couldn't text him. I'd call his number and listen to his voicemail, over and over again, staring at the walls.

How do people deal with grief? I distinctly remember saying something to somebody on the phone, a week after Peter died, in a calm voice, as I washed up the dishes. I said, I think this will be good for my art. My friend was in the other room and I saw a look of horror cross her face as I scrubbed the oil from the frying pan, the phone nestled in the crook of my shoulder.

I had left sex work when I moved to Sydney, sort of. I couldn't be Gia anymore. I cut my hair into a short fringe and shaved the underneath. I wore it up high, the cold wind tickling my bare scalp. I lived in a huge photographic studio, a warehouse, with two other guys. We had no insulation, so it was either boiling hot or freezing cold. Sometimes I would go into my room and play music to drown out the sound of my crying but I'm sure they heard me. I took a lone weekday shift at a rub and tug in Cronulla. I'd be lucky to make a few hundred bucks, which I'd carefully budget to pay my rent and for groceries.

So I had this idea that I'd channel my grief into my art. I'd sit up all night, cutting pieces from old books I'd find at thrift stores and XXX magazines from the sex shops in Kings Cross. I'd paste and cut until my fingers were gummy and peppered with sharp little paper cuts.

One night when I was home alone, I heard banging and shouting coming from the door. I sat in my room, paralysed with fear. The shouting was muffled, words indistinguishable. The pounding grew louder. My heart was in my throat. I crawled from my bedroom to the lounge room and hid behind the sofa. I heard the footsteps travel back down the staircase and down the alley to the other door. I couldn't breathe, couldn't remember if I had locked that door. My hands shook as I dialled the number of Redfern police. *Somebody is trying to break in*, I whispered down the line. The police officer stayed on the line with me as they sent two officers to the warehouse. *Hurry*, I remember saying to him.

I could see the red and blue lights flickering through the window and then there was a knock on my door. The voice on the phone assured me it was a police officer, so I opened it. They were standing with two young guys, both of them really good looking, I remember that distinctly.

'These two told us they have an appointment here, something about a meeting with the owner?' The police officer looks at me.

The two guys stand there awkwardly.

'Yeah, we are meant to be meeting Sam.'

Relief is replaced quickly by fury.

'What the fuck is wrong with you both? What kind of fucking maniac bashes at the door like that? You scared the fucking shit out of me!'

Suddenly I'm looking at myself from afar. I'm in my pyjamas and I have no make-up on, tears are streaming down my face and my heart is racing and I know I look insane but I can't stop. I can't control my fear. I can't say, I'm sorry but I assumed you were coming in here to rape and kill me. I can't say, I'm sorry but the worst thing I could ever have imagined has just happened to me and now my life will always be me on the edge of my seat, waiting for nightmares.

I run to my room, throw the door shut. I look at all the collages on my walls. The collage of the twin fetuses in utero, their heads touching. The tiger with the cub between its jaws, in a jungle of green and psychedelic flowers. 1800 sex phone lines, garish yellows and reds cut out. *Young horny teen sluts for you, call now.* I stand there and I begin to rip them down, slowly at first but then I pick up the pace. I shred them to pieces with my hands, I turn them into a confetti that dances across the hardwood floors. I want to shit on a canvas, throw up on it, slice my fucking hand open, smear my blood on it and fire a gun through it, but even then I wouldn't be able to express how I feel. I can't get it out, the pain inside of me. It's eating away at me like a cancer.

I fall asleep surrounded by all my artwork from the last few months in pieces.

The next day, I call my dad. I need to come home, I say.

I have $400 left to my name. I spend $50 of that on a train ticket from Sydney to Melbourne. My friend Brad drives me to the train station, with my bags of linen and clothes. I spend twelve hours staring out of the train window, wondering how I got there. When I arrive at Southern Cross Station, my dad is standing on the platform.

———

I'm in my childhood home. My father's house. When I look out my window, I see galahs flock together in the nature reserve. Everything in the house is the same, except that sitting in the lounge room are big plastic tubs. Inside the tubs are my dead brother's possessions. My little brother Will and my dad collected them from his house. I go through his toiletries and I spray his cologne on me.

I visit my mother. She listens to me as I cry. She takes me to her bedroom and pulls down a plastic bag. Inside is my brother's favourite sweater. She tells me she wrapped it in the bag to keep the smell in. We take turns breathing it in.

I sometimes get a little bit of pot and roll myself a skinny joint, which I smoke at the park next door. I get stoned and sit on the swings, my jacket bundled close to my body for warmth. It works for a while. But one night, as I come back in from getting high, I see all my dead brother's possessions in the lounge room. On top of the coffee table is the booklet from his funeral. I walk over and pick it up, and stare at his face on the front cover. I begin to feel a cold sensation in my chest, and it dips into my stomach. I am starting to trip out. Peter is dead I think, and I'm going to die one day. What happens when you die? What will it feel like? Will I feel like I can't breathe, will I be gasping for breath, clawing at the sides of my bed under the fluorescent hospital lights? Will it be a car that knocks me over and I'll bleed out on the side of the road? Then I start to think about time, how big the universe is, and I try to comprehend the fact that both are infinite. Or perhaps it's finite, and if you go to the end of the universe it's just white, empty space. I try to think about what I could do to break up my acute awareness of my own mortality and I decide I'll fold the laundry. Socks are fucking weird, I think, my hands starting to feel like they belong to another person. My little brother comes home from work and finds me red eyed, crouched in the corner of the laundry, weeping over mismatched socks.

I go back to the strip club. I buy myself a pair of stripper heels with my cafe pay and I take two buses and a tram to work. I roster myself on for four nights a week. I work Wednesday, Thursday, Friday and Saturday. I develop a work routine that becomes regimented and structured in a way I've never had before. I wake up, make myself a coffee and smoke cigarettes as I read the news and scroll through my phone. I shower and shave every part of my body. I reapply my fake tan in the bathroom with music playing. I lay down a towel in front of the mirror on my wardrobe, turn on my little heater and lay out my make-up. I sit cross legged and stark naked I slowly transform my face. Dramatic winged eyeliner, two pairs of false lashes stacked on top of each other. I pack my stripper suitcase—bikinis, stripper heels, a pack of baby wet wipes, marshmallow scented Chi Chi perfume from Target, gum, my sparkly body powder with fluffy puff to dab onto my skin, a purse to hold my cigarettes and money in. I put on my leggings and sweatshirt, sweep my black hair into a bun and clip on my ass-length ponytail. I take the 3:30 p.m. bus to The Pines shopping centre where I grab a latte, then I take the 4:10 p.m. bus to the city. I walk from the bus stop to the tram, where I stand next to people in suits. I am bedazzled from the neck up. Often, I get to work at 6:30 p.m. and I beat the manager there. I wait on the steps patiently and smoke. I have nowhere else to be.

When you are the new girl at a strip club, you keep your head down and mind your own business. You can smile tentatively at the same girls you see each shift, but you don't speak unless you're spoken to. You'll get friends once you earn your stripes, once they see you coming in night after night. You don't take the mirror area where one of the girls always sits. You don't strike up a conversation with the top earners. You wait it out; you do week after week of not speaking to anyone or having somebody to laugh about a customer with, or someone to check if your tampon string is hanging out. Then, suddenly, one day you'll come to work and put your suitcase down and look in the mirror and a girl will make eye contact with you and say, 'Hi.' Then she'll say she likes your bikini, and you'll compliment her on her shoes. Then the next shift you'll ask each other how your day was. A few weeks later, you walk into work and you find your group of friends by the bar and you sit down with them, and you think, I really love my job.

I bought an ebook about stripping for $20 online promising that I'd grow rich if I follow the steps.

The first step is to set your money goal. On a weeknight, when it was slow, I wanted to make $500. On a weekend, when it picked up, I set my money goal as $1000. One of my friends told me about the power of repeating a mantra before a shift. I would go and stand in the bathroom after I got dressed and I'd repeat to myself in the mirror, *tonight will be a good shift. I will make the money I want. I will have fun, the night will go past quickly, and I will leave here feeling good.* I would say it to myself until I believed it and then I'd saunter out of the bathroom and find my first customer.

The second step is to get your first dance out of the way as quickly as you can. The book said to find a spot in the club where you can always see who's walking in the door. I would position myself at a chair by the bar, and I'd watch the guys walk in. I'd give them enough time to buy a drink and then I'd go over and introduce myself.

Third step—don't pitch too quickly. Don't make the customer feel like you're coming to hustle him (even though that's exactly what you are doing). You walk over and ask if that seat's taken, make up something about needing to rest your feet. Kick a leg up and show them how high your stripper heels are and crack a joke. Lean in, ask them how their day's been. Spend at least five minutes trying to form connections between the two of you. You've vacationed in that spot too, you also like that album. Take your perfectly manicured hand and place it on their wrist to admire their watch, let them know you like the way they dress. Wow, you say, leaning in close so they can smell your perfume and minty breath, you just have the bluest eyes I've ever seen.

You can sit on their lap but that won't always work. You've let them touch you for free and now they will see how long they can have you there without spending a dollar. Take your hand and place it on the back of their arm (it's comforting and non-threatening) and ask them in a breathy voice, want me to get naked for you? Or you can say, want to go and play? Or, want to watch me take these clothes off? Whatever you do, don't stand there with your arms crossed, snapping your gum and spit out, wanna go for a dance? Because the answer will always be no.

Take them by the hand as they follow you into the lap dance room. Don't talk about the money until you're strad-dling them as they sit on the couch, or the chair, or the sofa. With your arms on their shoulders and your boobs at their eye level, ask them if they want the fun dance or the boring dance. The fun dance, you say, tracing your fingers down your body, is where you can touch me, and I'll grind in your lap. The fun dance is $100. They almost always pick the fun one.

Always tip the DJ—this should be step four. If you don't tip the DJ, bring them drinks. Say hi to them when you walk in. If you make friends with the DJ, you won't get stuck doing your stage show to Nickelback. My three songs were always 'Long Cool Woman (in a Black Dress)' by The Hollies, 'Closer' by Nine Inch Nails and 'Pour Some Sugar on Me' by Def Leppard. I bought myself a pair of thigh-high patent leather boots. This is a stripper trick—the boots have enough grip that you can climb the pole and dangle from the roof without the core strength of a Russian gymnast. When you get on stage, turn it up. Make every pair of eyes in that room turn to you. Crawl across the floor, spin around the pole, lie on your back and spread your legs. Make eye contact with each guy sitting at the stage. Flick your hair, sweep the floor, roll your hips. Don't half ass it. Don't slow down, don't stop and think about it. Just keep going. Stuff all your notes into your purse and keep track in your mind, get addicted to the feeling of a guy opening his wallet. When you finish your shift, sweaty and your make-up half running down your cheeks, sit on the toilet, take each note out and unfold it in your lap. Run your fingers along the notes and stack them together. Be pleasantly surprised that there's an extra $100 in there that you forgot about.

The strip club became my life. I wanted to escape my own more than I could explain. I needed a place that felt like I wasn't just floating adrift, alone and lost. When I walked into work and people remembered my name, I held on to that feeling all night. When my work friends squealed hello and opened their arms to embrace me, I held on for a beat longer. I became friends with the bouncers, and I'd smoke a cigarette with them at the doorway, cracking jokes. The server at Nando's across the road knew me by sight, because every night I'd come in around 8 p.m. for hot chips with chicken salt. They'd reach into the fridge and pull out my chip dip without me having to say anything. The nights I worked flew past in a blur of lap dances, cans of Coke, cigarettes, spritzing marshmallow perfume on my neck, baby wiping my pussy between dances.

One night I came to work, and the manager was at the bar. He said something, I don't remember what, or who to. But I felt the floor disappear underneath me and my heart plummet and I ran into the change rooms and started sobbing. Perhaps he said something that made me feel like I didn't fit in, maybe it was an inside joke I wasn't privy too, but in that moment I felt like I had been thrust out into the cold. Didn't they understand, I thought to myself, wiping snot off my runny nose in the change rooms, that this place was all I had? I thought they understood that I was a stray who had been taken into this new family, one I needed so badly.

Vietnam

Will and I are standing in the pouring rain, huddled under a scrap of tin roof that's just keeping the drops of water from our cigarettes. Our backpacks on, and each carrying a plastic shopping bag with cold water, sweet biscuits, bottles of iced tea.

The town of Hội An bustles past us as we hurry to finish our cigarettes before we embark on our eighteen-hour bus journey. I am filled with a sudden rush of love, for the bright red plastic chairs where people sit and eat steaming pho, for the smell of the wet asphalt from the rainy season, for the rides clutching my brother's back on a scooter and for feeling alive again.

We are taking a sleeper bus: a single seat each that reclines backwards with just enough room to stow our passports and laptops beside us as you try to sleep. We throw our suitcases in the luggage compartment underneath and begin to set up our sleeping quarters. I dole out the Valium from the packets we've bought at the pharmacy, over the counter, only $5 for 50. Full-strength ones and we are going to need them, because the bus drives at breakneck speed through the pitch-black night and we feel every pothole and crack in the road.

It's midnight and my brother and I sit at a roadside cafe, smoking cigarettes and eating a bowl of broth with greying pieces of chicken floating in it. The floor is an ashtray, my eyes feel sandy, but I've grown used to using the bidet in the toilets and I'm beginning to understand the language more. I am glad to be here, among these other travellers.

My brother gently shakes me awake, and we grab our things and stand on the side of the road in Nha Trang. It's 6 a.m. but a cafe has just opened its shutters. The two of us sit side by side, eating hard-boiled eggs in crusty baguettes, sweet coffee made with condensed milk, smoking more cigarettes. My brother and I have grown to travel together intuitively, sensitive to when the other is weary or homesick, feeling the same rush as we fall further in love with Vietnam. Our final bus trip takes us along the coastline to our destination of Mũi Né and we watch as the electric blue sea darts between the leaves of banana trees and palms. Shacks dot the highway, precariously clinging to cliffs.

We are sitting at a beachside cafe. At the start of the day we had grand plans to sightsee but wound up at this sleepy little hippy place with its own treehouse, complete with bean bags and a rickety ladder. We sit across from each other, reading books, doing Sudoku puzzles and drinking cocktails. We get drunk and watch the sun sleepily.

My little brother has escaped to Vietnam many times since our brothers died. He tells me about his first trip. It was just after James died. As the plane landed he felt tears well up and begin to run down his cheeks. He sobbed quietly as the plane made its way to the gate. The friends he was travelling with were quiet, understanding. Perhaps they sensed my brother's ambivalence, both his deep sorrow and profound relief to be able to escape from what had happened. This is the first time he cries in Vietnam.

He tells me about the day he is walking across town, on his way to get a coffee from his favourite cafe in the city. As he is paying, he hears loud chanting and the sound of a drum beating from the street. He walks outside to see a procession trailing by. A religious ceremony, he assumes. People throw flower petals. A monk cloaked in yellow robes leads the way. Banners with Vietnamese script are carried by the women walking alongside. An entire family on a single scooter drives slowly, weaving through the procession. There is music and sound and an air of festivity, but something is different and he can't place it. My brother stands to the side, and then he sees the coffin being carried. An altar and candles. He begins to run, his coffee spills, and he can't breathe or think properly. He wonders about how different it would be to celebrate the life, to mourn in a way that allowed for recognition, to be able to weep in public. This is the second time he cries in Vietnam.

The third time he cries in Vietnam, a hot wind blows over the sand dunes of Mũi Né, making us restless and irritable. We snap at each other. We walk away. A match is struck and thrown into the gas and the two of us explode. We slam doors, hurl insults at one another. I throw a cigarette lighter at my brother's head. He calls me a bitch. Then I see his face crumple, and he folds down into himself and places his head in his hands and begins to sob. I wrap him in my arms, and I feel a rising anxiety that threatens to overpower me. I want to run. I want to escape.

He is sick. He can't eat properly. When he lived in Hội An, it rained for two months straight and he felt like he was going insane. He is running out of money. He doesn't know what he wants to do with his life. His plan to stay and teach English in Vietnam is fraught with bureaucratic issues and, most of all, he misses our brothers. He feels like he needs to be the fun person at the party, the one who'll light your cigarette and tell you a joke, the first one on the dance floor, an ear to anybody who needs it, but he's collapsing under the pressure.

'I'm so depressed,' he tells me, and the wind blows his words so that they swirl around me, dancing through my head. I try to remain calm because if I give in, all hope is lost. But I'm so afraid I am going to lose him; I'm so scared he will be next to succumb to this disease that's wrapping its hands around him.

I make plans. I go into problem-solving mode. I tell him, you need to get help. You need to see somebody. You need to go home and face reality. A deeply selfish part of me needs him to go home because I need to escape. What I am telling my brother is what I'm too scared to tell myself.

One balloon

The first night, I don't have internet yet, or a couch. I push my mattress onto the floor in the bedroom and I put my sheets on it. I grab my purse and take the elevator down to Collins Street. JB Hi-Fi closes in 30 minutes. If I hurry, I can make it.

I walk the DVD aisles. The store lighting is harsh and bright, reflecting back off the shrink-wrapped DVDs. I look at my hands as they touch the plastic, and I wonder who they belong to. I haven't felt inside my body since James died. I feel as though I've climbed inside the skin of this person called Rita and I am living her life. When I talk to people, I can hear a stranger's voice speaking. When I touch things, it feels like I am operating a robot's hand, sending a computer signal to my brain. When I spend too long thinking about these things I feel like I might start screaming. I try to stop the thoughts. The thing I am most afraid of is screaming. I pay for my DVDs and I walk home. On the way, I stop and get a pack of sushi which I know I won't be able to eat. I should be celebrating. I've escaped. I got away from Danny.

———

I met Danny when I moved to Brisbane. We matched on Tinder and in between bookings, I would rush to my phone and I'd read the paragraphs he'd send me back. Danny was funny, he was deep, he was eloquent, and I drank in every word he said, read the lines he'd send me twice over. I'd feel butterflies in my stomach when his name popped up on my iPhone.

On our first date, Danny and I had a fight. I went to his apartment in Fortitude Valley. It was chic and well decorated. Danny had a box of wine that he received every month from a wine club. He chose a bottle for us to drink and I thought this was sophisticated. I began to feel inadequate and small. As we spoke and Danny became funnier and more charismatic, I shrank into myself. I became drunker, I picked a fight with him and when I got into the taxi I began to cry. I wanted Danny to like me so badly, and I didn't understand why.

He gave me a second chance. On our next date I apologised and he told me he thought I was weird, but he was curious and wanted to know more about me. We had lunch together and talked and as we walked down the street in the Valley, Danny took hold of my hand and didn't let it go.

Danny was into BDSM too. He would text me long para-graphs from work, telling me about how he wanted to break me into a thousand little pieces and put me back together again. How he wanted to fuck me slowly with his hand on my throat and choke me until I passed out, kissing me softly the entire time. He told me how special I was to him, how I made him feel things he hadn't felt since his ex-wife. Danny said to me that I was the only woman he had wanted to spoon in a long time.

The first time Danny made me come, I was lying in bed next to him. He pinned down my arms and pushed his fingers inside me and told me I was his good little girl as he rubbed my clit. I couldn't move if I had wanted too. On the stereo, The Growlers. He looked me in the eye and said to me that every time he heard those lyrics, he thought of me. Afterwards, he gave me his black American Express card and I walked across the street to get our morning coffees. I was sleeping at Danny's house almost every night. In the evenings, when we were outside in the balmy summer night air, I would sit on the ground and Danny would sit in his seat. I sat at his feet like an obedient dog.

———

I am very afraid of the window in my new apartment. The apartment on the eleventh floor of a high-rise, and I don't have a balcony. It is a small dwelling, with a study, a kitchen and lounge room that are connected and a bedroom that's

*separated by the door. Windows run along the entire back
of the apartment and the blinds don't shut properly. I think
about how it would feel to let myself fall out of the window,
as I sit on the edge of the sill to smoke, the DVD playing the
menu screen music on repeat.*

———

I'm housesitting for my friends. I am looking after their
French bulldog for two weeks. Four nights a week, from
6 p.m. till close, I strip at a club. When I get home, the dog
sits at the door of the shower and follows me around the
house before curling up at my feet on the bed as I go to
sleep. The silence of the house frightens me.

I don't know what to do with my days off, so I walk the
dog to a cafe and I sit there. Each morning when I wake up,
for a few seconds I forget Peter is dead. This is my favourite
part of the day. I think the hole inside me has its own gravitational pull. I see Danny's name pop up on my phone and
my stomach drops. How did he know I needed him?

Danny and I go for dinner. He has moved to Melbourne.
He has sold his apartment. He doesn't have a black American
Express card anymore, and he will be moving into a share
house in Coburg. He works at a call centre. I decide none of
this information is important, and when he says, Rita, I love
you, let's get back together, I say, OK.

Danny says the only way we can be together is if we live
together straight away. I need to leave my dad's place and

come move in with him. He doesn't have a bed yet. I take care of everything. I go to Target; I use my stripping savings to buy us new sheets. I organise the removalist and I don't say thank you to my father. I leave my keys in the mailbox. I need to be with Danny now. I don't stop and consider that Danny giving me an ultimatum on our first date in a year was strange. I run to be by his side.

The house is dark and dingy. The hot water runs out quickly. Our roommates are stoners and the kitchen is never clean. The days of boxes of expensive wine and sitting in the courtyard are behind us but I believe I am building something with Danny and that I am investing in him. I have my first drink in nine months. Danny encourages me to break my sobriety.

For a while, things with us are good. Danny gets home from work and I sit in the kitchen and roll him a joint. I've already started cooking dinner. We laugh and we play, and Danny has me in stitches as I'm chopping up vegetables. He and I have debates and we talk intensely with each other; he tells me how much he appreciates me. He tells me this job is temporary and he will go back to engineering. We talk about our future, the family we want to have. When we lie in bed and Danny is fucking me, he tells me he wants to get me pregnant. He says he's going to buy me a house and we will have a dog and I'll drive a Range Rover. I believe him. The fear I felt with him when he first opened the door to his apartment is gone. We feel like equals now.

I don't remember when the bad times started. There were fights. Arguments that began quietly but eventually woke up the whole house. Screaming. Crying. They always ended the same way, with me begging Danny to forgive me for whatever it was I had done that day. Inside I knew I was back where I thought I'd never be again, I was back with Todd. This time I didn't have Peter to call. I don't have James to drive over and kick in the door. Danny had felt like a lifeboat in the ocean I was drowning in. I take Danny with me to see my therapist and we try couples counselling. Danny is warm and charming, and sometimes he agrees to try the ideas she recommends to us. Other times, he mocks them. 'Oh,' he says, 'you're using "I Feel" statements, again.'

I remember the worst one.

'Get in the house.' I go into the bedroom, and my heart is beating so fast. Danny rolls a cigarette, standing over me as I crawl onto the mattress we share, where we fuck, where we laugh.

'Things were better,' Danny screams at me, 'when you sat at my feet like a fucking dog.'

'You don't realise,' he says, 'how fucking lucky you are to have me.' Danny drags on his cigarette and I watch the ash drop onto the floor, as he rolls it between the fingers that caress me and fuck me. I flinch with each word.

He reaches for the ashtray. He turns and plugs his iPod in, methodically scrolling though the songs. He savours each moment, knowing that I won't move, that I can't move.

'I'm sick of the people we live with having to listen to this shit.' He's made a decision to stop our housemates from hearing who he is. He turns back to me. His face is close to mine.

'You aren't special, Rita. You're a cunt.'

I close my eyes tight.

I try to beg for forgiveness. 'I know I'm shit!' I scream, striking my hands against the bannister of my bed, feeling the blue bruises bloom like pansies across my skin. I will make my penance.

'Get on the fucking bed. You can choose to leave and not take it, but if you do, you will never speak to me again.' He already knows what I'll choose.

I crawl across the bed, my face between my hands. I can hear him undo his belt; he walks to the bed. This isn't sex. It is punishment. I would have preferred he had just punched me in the face, an action I feel I wouldn't have played a role in accepting. I allowed him to beat me.

'Come to the edge of the bed.'

I can't remember how many times I felt the belt strike my ass.

I crawl to the edge of the bed. I burn myself twice with my cigarette. I'm sobbing and I just want it to be over. I want Danny to feel he's won.

'Go tell your friends I beat you!' he says, putting his face close to mine. I can feel his breath, the hatred in his voice. He shoots to kill. Danny knows right where to aim when it comes to me because I've told him everything.

'Everybody will get sick of your shit, Rita. One day, you'll be old and ugly and nobody will care anymore.'

Later that night Danny holds me in bed as I cry.

'You know I love you,' he says, 'even with how you are. I still love you.'

———

Here the timeline begins to get confusing. Did Danny beat me after James died? Or was it before? When did I stop eating? Was it after the funeral? Was I cutting myself then? Did Danny and I ever really have fun? When did I sign the lease for the apartment? Did Danny help me sit the STAT test or had I already left him? Why is it that I can only remember that motel room in Glen Waverley, my first booking back as an escort? I can see the bricks on the walls and I remember that I ordered salmon and vegetables from room service, but I don't know anything else.

I can't remember.

Here are the fragments. There's a shoot in Sydney, a week after James died, for my escorting photos. Danny didn't come to the funeral because he couldn't get an Uber. As they walked out with James's coffin, I saw his friends' faces crumple but mine didn't. I couldn't cry. I didn't feel anything.

When did Danny beat me? Was it before or after?

The coffin was being put in the back of the hearse. As it was being slid in, I heard my mother say *that's my little boy* and she begins to cry. I still don't cry.

My friend is there. She is holding my hand because Danny couldn't get an Uber. She came at the last minute. The procession goes down a long road and there is a car there which I climb into. I can't walk and see those people; I don't know how to use my legs. But I can see my mother and my father has her in his arms and she is leaning on him, and as the car starts to move I say, stop. Let me out.

The bagpipes start and a man shouts something, and I see everyone raise their hand in a salute. My best friend is holding me and I still haven't cried. *But we just did this,* I say to myself.

————

I didn't know what it was called until a year or so later. I needed to know what the song was so I went through Spotify, typing in the words bag pipe. I remember the melancholy, each song sounding like loss, like how my heart felt but none was right. I knew how to find my feelings and my memories and the only way I could bring them out was to hear the music from the funeral. Everything else was lost to me—smells, images. So I clicked song after song until I recognised it, and then I fell to my knees on the tiles of the shower. I could turn the shower on and that way, nobody would hear me cry.

————

I am so skinny, I think to myself, as I look at my body in the mirror of the bathroom in the apartment that Danny found.

I can see my ribs. Danny says something to me as we eat the dinner I've made and I can't finish it. I push away my plate, and I keep pushing them away. Picking at the vegetables, mashing the rice into neat little squares, scraping it all in the bin at the end.

———

I'm in the apartment Danny found and I know he called me a fucking bitch. A traitor. He found the apartment. I turned to Danny, as I loaded the last box into the removalist truck, and said, *it's my fucking money.*

———

My friend Tara and her boyfriend have broken up. I suggest she lives with me, in the spare room. Sometimes when I'm talking to Tara, I notice my hands are shaking. They have been doing that a lot lately. I am so grateful for her company. It reminds me that I am alive and that I exist on this mortal plane.

Without Tara there, I feel like a single balloon floating above earth.

Danny comes over one night. I don't know why I asked him to. He starts shouting at me and I'm crying and I've forgotten that Tara is at home. She comes out of her room and her dog is barking at Danny and she says that she *thinks he needs to leave.*

I remember that I am picking up things off the floor. Little presents, individually wrapped. A crumpled card. It was

Danny's birthday. Tara helps me, but when I look at her, she looks back at me and I feel relief. She's seen it too. The monster he's hidden from everyone. Tara sees the bogeyman in the closet. I'm not alone anymore. I'm not crazy.

———

It's New Year's Eve. Tara and I are drinking champagne in the kitchen and I don't feel like I'm going to float away as much. We go out to the pub and sit with friends and laugh, and as the night goes on, my phone lights up with texts. They are from my friends. They come in varying levels, as people's pills kick in, as the champagne bottles empty. My friends tell me that they love me. That I am beautiful. And I am special. That they feel lucky to have me, and that they wish me a happy new year. As I read the texts I feel the tears rolling down my cheeks. At first I think I am happy, but then I realise how I feel is surprised. I am surprised I am lovable.

Room 7

I'm in Room 7, the one everyone says is haunted, at the shitty brothel in the outer suburbs of Sydney. It's a few months after Peter died. All the girls say that, at night-time, you can hear creaking noises in the room. And that the lights flicker. Nobody wants to work in that room. My client is morbidly obese. He makes a heaving, rasping sound as he breathes. His lungs are compressed by the weight of his chest. He is covered in psoriasis and there is a thick, oozing sore on his side that's covered with gauze. I can see fluid leaking onto the white bandage, yellowing the edges. He lies back on the bed and as I undress his breathing grows urgent. His little eyes follow me around the room. He has paid me for a standard booking—just a massage, a fuck, a hand job and a blow job with the condom on. As I straddle his naked body, I have to heave one leg over to get to the other side.

I'm searching for his cock inside the rolls of his stomach flesh, and as I slide on the condom, he grabs my arms and tries to pull my face towards his. His voice is nasal and thick.

'Give me a kiss, love.'

'I'm sorry babe, kissing is extra. Do you have another $50?'

He grunts and sighs, and tries to pull me close again, his sharp nails digging into my forearms.

'I'm on the pension love, I can't afford it. Can't you make an exception?'

His breath reeks. I sidle away from him, start giving him a blow job. I want to cry, I want to run screaming from the room. I'm blowing him and I think to myself, if I ever believed in a god or anything, he doesn't exist in this room. Where are you Peter, I ask myself, and look up. The lights flicker off and on, off and on.

Florist

My mother and I decide to visit the graves on the weekend. I am trying to be a better daughter. We meet at her place, and we drop into the florist on the way.

I pick out bright pink gerberas, and the florist asks me if I want them wrapped. I don't know why I say yes, why I deliberate over the coloured tissue paper or what greenery to add to the bunch.

As she bundles the flowers up, we make small talk.

'Are these for a friend?'

'No. We are going to visit my brother's grave.' I decide to not let her know it's 'brothers' plural. I feel it's inappropriate to burden people with so much death.

'Oh,' she replies. Then, 'Which cemetery?'

'Warrandyte,' I reply as I browse the gift cards.

'Oh, I've had quite a few people come in today who are going there.'

'Oh.'

Mum and I drive out to the cemetery. Today is the first time I will go and see my siblings' graves. I have told myself it's because it's too far away for me to travel. I hope that seeing earth and trees and knowing only their ashes in the ground exist rather than ghosts will stop the madness from eating away at my brain.

I am afraid I will die next. I am standing on the edge of the abyss and each time I look into the darkness it crooks its finger at me and beckons me in. Come join us, it says. Stop trying. It's easier here.

Mum and I place the flowers in Peter's vase in his memorial plaque. James's plaque is still being made.

'It's like I'm in a play,' she says, staring out at the lawns. 'A horrible play that the curtain never closes on.'

I sit down on the bench and feel tears drip onto my cheeks. We hold hands, our only consolation today knowing that somebody else is lost in this madness too.

Why did they do it? Did they regret it? Our thoughts run around in maddening circles. All of us are left, asking the same questions. At every family gathering we try to speak of pleasantries and end up back puzzling over the same riddles. *Why. How. Why. How.*

There's one thing we never ask. Whose fault is it? But the question is etched all over my mother's face as she pulls out the small watering can and pair of scissors she brought with her, tending to my brothers as she did all their lives, and now in their deaths.

As we walk back to the car, she turns to me. The sun beats down on us and the nearby eucalyptus offers no shade, nowhere to hide from truths.

'Sometimes, Rita,' she says, 'I wish I could just dig a hole right here beside them and lay down in it. Sometimes, I really do.'

PTSD

I've never been very good at letting go. I hold friends and old lovers like cards to my chest. I finish fantasy books and spend the day wondering what happened to the people in the pages, searching the internet for answers in fan fiction forums. People I was close with once receive a message from me in the middle of the night, words flowing freely from the wine I've been drinking. I have a box in my cupboard and inside are polaroids of me, with an ex-boyfriend's cock in my mouth or my arms around an old best friend. I keep receipts and ticket stubs and matchbooks from hotels I've stayed in. I don't know why I struggle so much to say goodbye to things.

I flew to Sydney two days after James died. I had spent my weeks in the brothel in Port Hedland planning my escort photoshoot. I'd bought all my outfits and paid for the hotel room. I drifted through the airport and into Darling-hurst. The photos were beautiful but if you look closely at my eyes, you can see they are staring at nothing. A beautiful, vacant doll.

'I can't believe you managed to come out of that,' people would say to me. It's unusual to have one older brother commit suicide, let alone two within an eight-month period. I smile and say, I didn't have a choice. There was no option but to forge ahead, put one foot in front of the other. My soul had left my body and it floated alongside me. It would lean into me as I woke each morning, in my new apartment, with my new escorting photos and it would say, look at your hands. They are separate from you, aren't they? Who controls them? I would wake each morning and be terrified of my own physical body, and the knowledge that I was in charge of it.

I rang my therapist every few days, unable to breathe. I wheezed down the phone, the panic constricting my throat.

'Jeanette,' I'd say, 'I think I'm going crazy.'

When I spoke to people it felt like we were underwater. When I heard my voice it sounded like it belonged to a different person, another entity called Rita. I became afraid of mirrors because when I looked at my reflection, I didn't know who that person was. I thought she was pretty, but she didn't feel like me.

One foot in front of the other. I walked each morning from my apartment on Collins Street to the Virgin Active Gym.

With each step, I reminded myself of my physical connection to the earth. I am not floating when I touch cement. I am not floating in Pilates class or when I squat and press kettlebells above my head. I need to stitch myself back inside my own skin to remind me I am in control of something.

Lack of control becomes something I think about a lot. Peter's suicide was controlled, James's was not. He went to his gun cupboard and then he walked the recommended distance away from ammunition and shot himself. All over in a few moments, a split-second decision. I wonder if I am so scared of my physical body because I believe I can't control it.

My brothers are dead, I say to myself every morning, hoping that it feels real and concrete like the pavement. It does not.

PTSD, I thought, was reserved for people who had been to war. Those who had been imprisoned, those who had been tortured. That felt like a real problem, and I felt guilty for having developed the disorder myself. I felt like an imposter. I didn't tell any of my friends what was really wrong with me. I hoped they wouldn't notice the way my hands constantly shook or that I often couldn't unlock my gaze from the walls, upon which I saw images of twin coffins being lowered into the ground.

I drifted. In and out of bookings, where, funnily enough, I was the best escort I'd ever been. I was such a blank slate of human behaviour that I was able to play act like I'd never been able to before. Before a client walked in, I'd go to my bathroom and practise facial expressions. I'd fix a smile on my face and hold it there the entire booking. When they left I'd go back to the window ledge, open another packet of cigarettes and lean out the window to chain-smoke, my face blank.

One of my clients is growing more existential each time I see him. He tells me of his struggles with his Jewish faith and his increasing fear that there is no afterlife. He looks at me with terror in his eyes as he reaches his conclusions. I stare back with my beautiful, vacant eyes. I don't say to him, I long for oblivion. I wish the darkness would swallow me whole so I can stop waking to my shaking hands, checking to see if it still feels like I'm not in my body.

———

I take an Uber home from a booking. The driver is short, his head barely higher than the steering wheel. On his lap is a *Dungeons and Dragons* player's handbook. A cluster of crystals dangle from the rear-view mirror. Lately I am silent in Ubers but this man's energy is so calming. He brings me joy with his adornments and his excitement about tabletop gaming. I think, I could be happy again, one day. As we talk he makes a turn for the freeway at City Road in South Melbourne. There is a loud thumping sound and then, a long, high-pitched scream reverberates through the car.

I look out of the back window and I see the faces of people staring at us. Their expressions frozen, fear in their eyes. I feel the cold grip of panic wash through me. The first thing I think is that there is a madman and he has a sniper rifle. He is about to shoot me in the side of my head through this back window and my brains are going to smear the windscreen and the pages of the *Dungeons and Dragons* book. I am going to die, I think. I freeze.

While I'm confronting my fate of being shot by a lone gunman at 3:30 p.m. on a Tuesday next to the freeway, my driver has pulled over. He races out of the car and I look behind me to see a pile of white fluff and a woman clutching a lead with no dog on the end. Her friend, standing beside her, has her own dog, still on the lead. She is screaming.

My first thought is, what kind of fucking idiot walks a dog near a freeway? I feel a deep sadness for my Uber driver, who made me feel hopeful that I could be happy again. He killed a dog because somebody was stupid and when he gets back in the car to finish the trip (at his insistence) his eyes are red from crying. I sit in the back, my hands clenched into fists. He tries not to cry as he drops me home. When I get out of the car, I call my mum and tell her what happened. The first thing she says is, what kind of idiot walks a dog near a freeway?

PTSD makes you cautious. It keeps you alert for threats, and it makes you think about every move you make. My mother and I couldn't comprehend the naivety of somebody walking their beloved pet near a six-lane highway. But we didn't notice when James and Peter didn't want to live anymore. Now we spend our lives watching and waiting.

I'm on the tram coming home and I see a backpack on the ground. PTSD makes me think that a suicide bomber would target an almost empty tram in the middle of the afternoon, two stops from my house. My heart races and I picture being burnt to death by shrapnel and hot metal that sears the flesh from my bones. I get up, my legs buckling, and I hit the stop button. I can barely hold it together. I feel the tears welling up in my eyes. I'm so embarrassed by my reaction as I walk home, watching the tram safely reach the depot without an explosion, but I can't let go of the ever-present fear—what if?

I wanted to live but what if? What if I succumbed to the darkness that snapped at my brothers' heels? I didn't know how suicide worked. Was it just that your brain snapped? Brain snaps and so many intrusive thoughts. Thoughts about chopping my fingers off with the chef's knife as I cook my dinner. Plunging my hands into the juicer. Saying FUCK very loudly in the middle of a packed tram. Leaning in and planting a giant kiss on a stranger's mouth as they hand me my change. Wrenching the wheel from the Uber driver and sending us plummeting off the bridge.

'Jeanette,' I say, 'I keep thinking these demented things. I need to be locked up.'

I accidentally wipe my old iPhone which has seven years of iMessage history between me and Peter. Oh well, I say to myself, in the grip of the blank, chilling calm I've grown accustomed to. I laugh with my friends and say, I could watch somebody be murdered with an axe and not bat an eyelid.

The funny thing about memories is that, when you put them inside a box and close the lid, they just come bursting back out. Sniper rifles aiming at my head. Screaming in public. Dead dogs. Car off cliff. Losing the last recordings I had of Peter's voice. Peter talking to me. Death. Suicide. I am out of control because I'm trying to control the memories. I thought the only way to go forward was to forget, because I knew I couldn't send a text to a ghost.

If they never existed then their deaths never happened and the pain I am in, the excruciating pain that forces my soul from my body, the pain that makes my brain say *chop off your fingers and feel it, you fucking coward*, doesn't exist. The only time I visit Peter and James is in my dreams.

I'm chasing James around street corners. He's ahead of me, my big brother, the oldest in the family. His blonde hair catches the sunlight and he tilts his head far enough back so I can just see his eyes and I know it's him. 'James,' I'm scream-ing at him, 'I need to talk to you.' His deep booming laugh as I fall behind. The laugh I remember from Christmases and birthdays, the one that would start in the car as he drove me, the laugh I'd hear when he was saying something I knew I shouldn't laugh at but did anyway. 'James,' I scream, 'come back here!'. He goes on laughing and I wake up.

Peter is in the car in the passenger seat, I reach for him from where I am in the back. I can feel the wool of his favourite jumper brush against me and I can smell him. His hand grips mine and he smiles at me and when I look ahead, I see the road is covered in gum trees, and sunlight is streaming through their leaves. I hold him tighter and tighter, and he's saying, you have to let go. I won't, and he tells me to look away, but I don't. I stare up at his face and it twists into scales and red eyes. A serpent's head. The snake opens its mouth and I see its long white fangs reach for my face. I start screaming and I'm back in my bedroom. I'm in my little apartment and it's dark, the screams flying out the window and down into the street below.

I go to Officeworks the next day and print out a photo. It's me, a newborn baby, swaddled. James holds me in his arms, sixteen and smiling proudly at the camera. Peter is next to James, his arm around his big brother. Peter is eight years old. They both look so excited to have me, their little sister. I frame it and place it on my bedside table.

The only way out is to remember.

My existential client sees the photo.

'Who's that?' he says, peering at the frame.

'Me and my brothers.' I pause. 'They are both dead.'

He stops bringing up death with me now.

Tiny bones

The first time I knew the world was a dangerous place I was sitting in a hotel room with my mum. My younger brother and my dad were out. We were on holiday in Vietnam, staying in Hanoi.

My dad's work allowed him to travel, and he believed in showing my brother and me the world, and for that I am forever grateful. I hope I can do the same for my own children someday.

In the hotel room, my mum and I are sitting on the bed. We are watching the Discovery Channel. I am maybe seven. Or perhaps I was watching it by myself, because I told her this story later on and she said, Rita, I would never have let you watch something like that.

It's a true crime documentary and it's set in a small American town, somewhere with red dirt and cacti and tumbleweeds. The narrator talks and up flashes a photo of a little girl who looks a bit like me. She has long blonde hair and it's pulled back with clips like my hair, like how my mother does my hair each morning. I watch in confusion. Why is her photo up?

She was removed from her front yard, and put into a van. The next shot is a close-up of tiny white bones, covered in red dirt under a clear blue sky. A shallow grave, dug in haste.

I experience my first panic attack. I run to my mum and I cry inconsolably, unable to breathe. All I can think about is how that girl must have felt, how afraid she would have been. I see her tiny bones in my dreams for weeks. I can still see them now.

'I would never let that happen to you,' says Mum, holding me close.

Our neighbours at Mum's house are a family—a husband, his wife and their three daughters who are older than us. There are six children in our family and lots of laundry. Mum asks us to take turns putting it out, and as you open the side door to the steps to go down to the line, you can hear screaming. Sometimes you hear crying, shouting. It trails down the side fence and into our yard. We hear it year after year. Our washing pile dwindles as the older children leave, move into share houses, or in with their partners.

'I think she's pregnant, one of the girls,' Mum says, as I'm putting the folded washing away on the shelves marked with each of our names. Peter's blue socks, James's football jumper, my sisters' Country Road jumpers. 'I hear her vomiting a lot now.'

Mum is outside in the front yard, near the fence, pruning her rose bushes with a pair of kitchen scissors. She hacks at the bushes and stares at him, the man who's always yelling, as he comes out to go to his car. She's sent my dad over there a few times, and even banged on the door herself. Nothing changes. The rose bushes bloom each year, the washing gets folded and the commotion continues.

And then it stops one day. We don't hear it anymore.

'I think he's dead,' says Mum, making dinner. 'Good.'

———

We are given a mobile phone to share, my little brother and me. My mum works and can't pick us up from school. Sometimes one of my older siblings who has their licence will collect us, but then my nan says, why don't they come here after school? I grew up less than a kilometre from my primary school, nan's house a block away. We have the phone and Mum tells us to call her, or Dad, or the police if anyone comes near us. We walk home. I'm in Year 4 and my little brother is in Year 2. We feel adult and responsible, our backpacks bouncing as we take the path beside the cricket oval, then down past the football field and up the hill and down the hill. Sometimes we dawdle; we talk to our friends at the school gates, and we chase each other around the oval.

We finally arrive at Nan's place and she throws the door open and bundles us into her arms. We are being squeezed to death.

'You little devils!' she says, as we squirm.

We would roll our eyes at Nan, who'd be ready to call the SWAT team if we took longer than fifteen minutes to get to her house. Now I understand. She sat there every day after school and hoped two blonde heads would appear at the end of her driveway, instead of one, or none. Tiny bones covered in red dirt.

As a teenager I have a phone, but I don't answer it. I come home from parties after midnight, smelling of pot smoke, the VCE jumper I took from lost property in my bag. I put it on at lunch and stroll out the school gates, cloaked in the uniform which means I'm allowed to go to Westfield for coffee and to get my nails filled. Nobody knows who I am anyway, a Year 10 student, another anonymous face in the thousands at my local high school. I turn the lock, gently shimmy the door open and walk into my dad's house and I see his bedroom light is still on, the door half open. He has to work the next morning.

'Reet,' he says, putting down his book. 'Answer your phone.'

Bigger bones in red dirt.

———

I'm in this house and this guy has all these enormous blow-up pool toys. I took the booking because I thought it was funny. They are speciality fetish pool toys imported from Germany, and they are made of soft vinyl. He tells me I'll become hooked on them, that I'll love the sensation against my bare skin. The house these pool toys are in is empty and mid-renovation, so black tarps hang against the windows. I walk in and feel very glad that my friend Julian is waiting in a car out the front. The client covers the pool toys in baby oil and we get naked and fool around on an orca that feels almost life sized. He moves my body around and gets closer to me. I'm fumbling on these pool toys and can't get a grip, can't manoeuvre my body skilfully like I usually would when a client moves his naked dick too close to me. I'm on all fours, bent over the tail and he presses his body against me, bearing his weight down. I panic. Nick flashes into my head, his weight on me, his cock in my ass. The black tarps are there and I go, am I about to be raped, and am I going to die? So I push him off me and I punch him, square in the stomach. I say to Julian in the car, as I run out of the house in leggings I've pulled on and my jumper, I don't know what came over me. I feel so embarrassed. But deep down I know what came over me. My will to live, at whatever cost. I would rather punch somebody who might have had innocent intentions than wait to find out it's too late, his hands closing around my throat, my last moments on earth on a rubber sex orca.

He texts me to apologise and I try to find a way to reply. I feel psychotic.

'Please understand,' I say, 'you are tall and strong and you are fucking me in an empty house with giant sex pool toys and that can send a really weird message to somebody who's already feeling a little on edge looking at *Dexter*-style tarps covering the windows.'

'I completely understand,' he replies. But how could he? How could he ever understand?

———

James told my mum about the sex work. We had a fight and he texts me, telling me I'm a junkie whore and a prostitute and he's embarrassed by me. He texts my mum and he tells her everything. I never told James about the work, but I told Peter and he told James. 'I hate James!' I scream, flinging my phone down. I deny and deny, telling my mother I dance at a strip club.

'It's not that I don't like . . . it, Rita,' she says, over a cup of tea in her kitchen. 'I just worry. I worry so much.'

Adult-sized bones, attached to flesh, inside a motel room, stuffed down a rubbish chute.

———

The day Peter died, he went to a motel room in North Melbourne and he lay down on a bed with the same kind of doona we would have laid on on a family holiday, listening to Kylie on his Discman. He put a needle in his arm and he left this world. My mother goes to his house that afternoon and she finds it clean, tidy. No note, his computer wiped clean. He even took out the recycling. The last gift he gave my mother was his clean home, and his body somewhere she'd never have to find it. While my mother stands in his house, a teenage girl gets off the bus a suburb away. A man gets off after her, a registered sex offender released on parole. He kills her. He leaves her body in the bushes. I find my mother, watching the news, the camera zooming in on the image of the girl's sobbing parents, parents who live down the road from us.

'I wish I could call them,' Mum says, staring at the screen. 'I wish I could let them know that I understand. That poor girl. Poor Peter.'

Christmas

At Christmas we were all together. I'd run to the door each time it rang, throwing myself onto whichever sibling had arrived. I'd grab them by the hand and drag them over to show them what Santa had brought me. The two recliners in the lounge room would be covered in gifts for me and my little brother, a chair each. I'd sit there and pore through all the pink things that were there, put on my new pyjamas.

My aunty had given me the Barbie Campervan, and James sat with me, helping to put it together. He stuck the stickers on the side and clicked the wheels in and I babbled away at him, putting my Barbies in to drive them around.

Peter sits next to me, and I have my new *The Little Mermaid* colouring book. I watch as Peter shows me how to colour in.

'You do it like this,' he says, pressing the pencils on the lines, creating a thin block of colour that he neatly shades in.

James and my sisters chase me down the hallway. I run away screaming because at the moment, their favourite thing is to pin me down and tickle me. They all crack up at me, me with this deep booming laugh. The sole purpose of tickling me is to hear how much I sound like an old man.

After lunch is over and Christmas is drawing to a close, I knock on Peter's bedroom door. I sit on the bed with him and he reads *The Rainbow Fish* to me.

———

One Christmas our cousins have grown older and created their own families, so it is just the six of us, my parents and my siblings' partners, their children. It's at James's house, and he's put a huge blow-up pool in the backyard. I'm twenty, one of the adults now. We all sit in the pool, drinking champagne and beers, my parents running after their grandchildren. I am in a hurry though, because I want to go to the party my friends are having. My dad is dropping me off at the station and he's given me a cooler bag full of bottles of Riccadonna sparkling. I wave goodbye to James and Peter and everyone and hurry out the door. Desperate to get away from my family.

———

There was just one more Christmas after that. My younger brother hosted it at my dad's house. He spent weeks organising the food, cleaning out the front yard, tidying my Dad's papers and things he'd scattered over the house. He told me, yelling down the phone, that he'd even bought cushions for the dining room set, that table usually covered in books, the seats so old they'd begun to sag inwards.

The divide was widening between me and my family. I was struggling to forgive my parents for things that had happened and things that had been said. I was struggling to forgive James for outing me to them. I was struggling with a drinking problem and a sense of anxiety I knew I wouldn't be able to control if I was around them, knowing that I was the outsider, the fuck up, the black sheep. I felt so strong in my community and felt they were the family I wanted and needed. I flew down from Brisbane, the place I've exiled myself to, not for Christmas but to see a guy.

My mother comes to my sister's house and we end up in an argument. She slaps me, I scream at her, and we end up rolling around the floor of my sister's lounge room, swiping at each other.

'I fucking HATE you!' I scream at her. 'I hate this fucking family!'

I call the guy I'm supposed to be seeing and his phone goes to voicemail, again and again. I'm meant to be having Christmas with him, with his family.

I stay at my friend's house and order Indian take-away from Menulog while her and her girlfriend do Christmas day together. I look on Facebook and see photos of my family, together, sitting in the sun. Will calls me, and he is so angry.

'You should be here,' he says.

Peter only stays a few hours before making an excuse to leave. We should have known then.

———

A new Christmas. I call my mother and tell her we can't have it at her house. It will be too sad, I say. We have to go on and make a new Christmas, a Christmas without Peter and James. We go to a buffet hall. There is a wishing well in the garden and a giant frog with water burbling from its mouth. It's hot and dusty. My mother takes a photo of us, the remaining children. We are all clinging tightly to each other, trying to smile. We all try so hard to make this day OK, but when we have finished our turkey and cranberry sauce and prawns, we are relieved. It is so painful for us to be around each other. The first Christmas photo without all six of our heads together, jostling each other, somebody complaining they didn't like the photo and *take it again, Mum*. We only needed one photo this year. Our bodies seized up, with the strain of trying to hold it together, to give our mother a Christmas. She told me later she didn't want one.

Nan

I pour the milk from the carton into the saucepan full of boiled potatoes, still in their skins. My hands move without needing to be prompted, to the pepper, the salt, the butter. I'm mashing and I remember how I learnt to do this—my nan showed me, in the kitchen at one of our family dinners. She told me to wait until the potatoes become little meringue peaks, any further and they turn to clag. I push my wrists down against the handle and as I do, I finally feel the tears roll down my cheeks.

I didn't cry at the funeral.

Our father, who art in heaven, hallowed be thy name, thy kingdom come . . . the words rolled off my tongue as we said mass in the chapel around the white casket. Out of all her grandchildren, my nan knew me the least. But it was me who was at the church first. I was smoking on the bench, waiting for everyone to get there. As the hearse pulled in, I felt uncomfortable. I shouldn't be the one greeting her. I make a joke about this to myself to hide the fact I feel regret. There are just so many of us and only one Nan. I didn't think there was any room for me.

Nan's casket looks like Peter's, but everything else is different. I don't remember the colour of James's casket. The burial rites are Catholic, and the words are about sins and the afterlife. I hold the crook of my aunt's arm as we sit outside in the sun. I am surprised when she tells me that she has lost her best friend, and I realise this is not a funeral for me. I am an outsider here. All I can do is squeeze her hand and be kind. I know what it's like to say goodbye to your best friend.

I eat spoonfuls of mashed potatoes as I sob. I think about my brother confiding in me beside the burial plot, his arm around mine. He said, I couldn't get close to another person again. I kept her at a distance because I didn't want to go through this again.

After Nan's funeral, I shut myself in the house for three weeks. I had my clients over for bookings and I smiled and chatted and drank coffee with them. I did not see my friends. I did not visit my family. I fucked strange men and I'd breathe a sigh of relief when they left. I'd go back to finding chores to do. Vacuum the floors, clean the skirting boards, wash my linen every day and spray lavender oil over it. My hair became greasy and my meals were just whatever was easiest. Toast. Beans. A tin of soup. I watch myself in the mirror when I fuck men and look if I can see my rib cage yet. The feeling of hunger is all I can control.

I got on the tram and sat there in silence. A man tried to get my attention, motioning for me to take my headphones off. I tried to laugh about it later, how I turned to him, ripped the headphones from my ears and screamed at him. I screamed at him and told him to go fuck himself, I felt every single hair of my body standing on end. My grandmother is dead, Peter is dead, James is dead and I was raped. I hope you get your fucking head kicked in, you stupid fucking cunt, I said. I stood up and towered over him with my fists curled into balls. I wanted blood. I wanted to bash that man's head against the bright green poles of the tram, I wanted to see his skull crack open. I got off the tram and my body shook and trembled. Not because I was scared but because I felt cheated out of the carnage I wanted.

Tonight I need to make mashed potatoes because I have to start caring for myself again. I have to start to eat again even though I don't want to. I have a collection of photos on my laptop and it's me in the same G-string, standing in front of the same painting, in the same light. I take it every few weeks to check. To make sure.

If my nan were here she would feed me, but I have to do it myself. She would roll out dough on her plastic mat and then fill a pie with chunks of beef and gravy. She would bring an apple pie over even though her hands were knotted and gnarled. She would have done that for me if I had asked but I didn't. I didn't ask because I didn't want her to know I was a prostitute and I couldn't get close to her because I didn't want to lie to her. I tell my younger brother this. He holds me tight and he says, she wouldn't have cared, Rita.

I eat the mashed potatoes alone in my apartment and I force myself to live again, to stop starving, to cry, to feel. I am not sad anymore because this was a normal death, a death at the end of a life full of love and children and warmth and happiness.

My grandmother was buried with my Pa, in the cemetery with my two brothers. As the two coffins meet, the silence in the cemetery is broken with a sound like the crack of a whip. I turn to see the sky full of birds, a chorus of cockatoo and galah voices fill the air as they fly out of the trees. My younger brother turns to me and I say to him, they are together again, and we smile. They are all together, I say to him, listen to them sing.

Epilogue

The tutor is starting the class. Everyone is back, it's a new semester. I'm slowly chipping away at my philosophy degree, a few classes each semester. Sometimes I skip lectures to take last-minute bookings or lie in bed, watching *Keeping Up with the Kardashians*. I make up for this free time by looking at abstracts until three in the morning, my eyes propped open by instant coffee and nicotine.

I roll out of bed and go to tutorials in a hoodie, sitting up the back, my long acrylic nails tapping away at the keyboard.

'Getting to know you' first-week tutorials are excruciatingly awkward, and I rehearse what I will say to the question, repeating it over and over in my head. I hope nobody recognises me from a porno I've done or a photo of my asshole on the internet.

The tutor asks each of us to say our name, and what school of thought, theory or philosophy we relate to or enjoy the most. I'm running through names in my head, trying to pick the one I believe suits me the most. I think of Jean Paul Sartre. I am Being, playing a role. I embody the role of the Prostitute, I play at being her. I know I am the sum of my choices, there is no God, no path predestined simply by the forks in the road I choose to take, snipping the thread of what could have been. I think about Erving Goffman, and the stigma I embody. I feel my deviant identity is simply a social construction, that what I do is inherently meaning-less, an act, two bodies meeting in an exchange. I think about Foucault and his panopticon, and the way I learnt to surveil my own body, staring at it in the mirror.

I am surprised that most people in my class identify as Nihilists.

Nihilism, in its philosophical definition, is:

> . . . the belief that all values are baseless and that nothing
> can be known or communicated. It is often associated
> with extreme pessimism and a radical scepticism that
> condemns existence. A true nihilist would believe in
> nothing, have no loyalties, and no purpose other than,
> perhaps, an impulse to destroy.*

It's so cavalier that it's laughable. I know real Nihilists—my brothers.

* https://www.iep.utm.edu/nihilism/

I don't usually say much in my tutorials, but today I turn around to speak to one of the men who raised his hand. 'Do you ever go on dates?' I say.

'Sure?'

'Do you ever go on Bumble? Tinder? What about girl-friends? Have you ever had one?'

The guys give me a weird look and some of them nod, or say yes.

'What about love? Have you ever loved someone, or something?'

I felt like I had proved something then, something I had believed but hadn't found the words for until this moment.

'Those statements contradict your beliefs,' I say. 'We all want to be loved. We all want to fuck. We all want to live and then we are all afraid to die. You assign value to these things, they give you purpose, they drive you forward. It's all we have. It's what life is. Lean into it.'

I turn back to my computer, legs crossed in my velour track pants, nails clicking on the keyboard.

Acknowledgement

First and foremost, I would like to thank my editor Kelly Fagan for believing in my writing and giving me the opportunity to tell my story.

I would like to thank each and every single person who bought my very first zine back in 2015, and supported my writing. Without you and your enthusiasm, kind words and support, this book wouldn't exist. I hope this book becomes successful and you can sell the original signed zines on eBay one day—and the nude polaroids I sent with them!

I would like to thank my partner, Anonymous, for being there during the mental breakdowns, crying, screaming, regressive episodes and for guiding me through the process of healing without a single complaint.

I would like to thank Clementine Bastow for the time she spent helping me find my voice within the beginning drafts at our 'office', aka the food court at Melbourne Central.

I would like to thank my therapist! You are really great at what you do!

To all my nearest and dearest on my secret Instagram account where I posted videos of me live blogging my nervous breakdown—thank you for listening, supporting and encouraging me when I felt like giving up.

Finally, I would like to thank all the sex work and queer activists—the people who made it possible and paved the way today for a hooker like me to write a book.